SCHOOLS OASIS

Poems of the Second World War

Edited by
Dennis Butts and Victor Selwyn

Editorial Advisers
Erik de Mauny and General Sir John Hackett

Educational Adviser
Dr John Rae

Nelson
in association with
THE SALAMANDER OASIS TRUST

Thomas Nelson and Sons Ltd
Nelson House Mayfield Road
Walton-on-Thames Surrey
KT12 5PL UK

51 York Place
Edinburgh
EH1 3JD UK

Thomas Nelson (Hong Kong) Ltd
Toppan Building 10/F
22A Westlands Road
Quarry Bay Hong Kong

Thomas Nelson Australia
102 Dodds Street
South Melbourne
Victoria 3205 Australia

Nelson Canada
1120 Birchmount Road
Scarborough Ontario
MIK 5G4 Canada

First published by Thomas Nelson and Sons Ltd 1992

ISBN 0–17–439682–1
NPN 9 8 7 6 5 4 3 2 1

Filmset by Wearset, Boldon, Tyne and Wear.
Printed in Hong Kong.

— War Poet —

I am the man who looked for peace and found
My own eyes barbed.
I am the man who groped for words and found
An arrow in my hand.
I am the builder whose firm walls surround
A slipping land.
When I grow sick or mad
Mock me not nor chain me;
When I reach for the wind
Cast me not down
Though my face is a burnt book
And a wasted town.

Sidney Keyes
March 1942

Note on The Salamander Oasis Trust

The collection of manuscripts, from which poems have been selected in this anthology, has been the task of The Salamander Oasis Trust, a registered charity (274654), founded in 1976 from among those who served and wrote in the Middle East in World War Two and took part in the original *Oasis* anthology, Cairo 1942/3. The Trust has published four anthologies (listed below), produced a tape of its poetry (National Youth Theatre direction, with Martin Jarvis, Irene Richard and others reading) and sponsored a television programme *War Poets of '39*, available on video. The Trust hands over all manuscripts collected to the Imperial War Museum in a special archive for students and historians of future years.

The Trust's activities have only been made possible by the generous support of benefactors, in particular, The Esmée Fairbairn Charitable Trust and Paul Getty Jr KBE.

The Trust's founders include G. S. Fraser and Professor Ian Fletcher, Erik de Mauny, John Rimington, Louis Challoner, Sir John Waller, John Cromer Braun, Victor Selwyn. Advisers: F. M. Lord Carver, General Sir John Hackett, Dr John Rae, Christopher Frere-Smith, Dennis Butts. Clifford Simmons and Gavin Ewart represent the Poetry Society on the Trust, prior to its eventual takeover of the *Oasis* poetry.

Contents

3 The Home Front

4 The Mediterranean and Italy

5 War in the Air

6 War at Sea

7 War in North West Europe: From Normandy to Berlin

Photographs and Illustrations

The Oasis anthologies
Return to Oasis (Shepheard Walwyn, 1980)
From Oasis to Italy (Shepheard Walwyn, 1983)
Poems of the Second World War: The Oasis Selection
   (Dent/Everyman, 1985)
More Poems of the Second World War: The Oasis Selection
   (Dent/Everyman, 1989)

Also available:
Oasis tape (C90 cassette) and *War Poets of '39* video (from BBC television)
from: Sussex Publications Microworld House 2–6 Foscote Mews London W9
2HH

Acknowledgements

The Salamander Oasis Trust gratefully acknowledges the continued support of the Esmée Fairbairn Charitable Trust, without which this anthology could not have been produced.

The Trust acknowledges, too, the interest of Alexander, Earl of Stockton, that facilitated publication. This joint venture has worked thanks to the enthusiasm of John Aldridge, Gill Stacey and Geoff Wadsley, in conjunction with the Trust's experience of four previous anthologies. As before, the Trust has enjoyed the benefit of its Advisers, F. M. Lord Carver, General Sir John Hackett, Dr John Rae and the very helpful staff of the Imperial War Museum, Roderick Suddaby, Phil Read, Mike Moody (documents and translation), Pauline Allwright (pictures and photographic). Jeremy Shearing, whose work is seen in the design and layout of the early OASIS anthologies, advised on typography and picture selections. Kenneth Gosling helped with proof-reading.

Dennis Butts thanks his colleagues at Reading University, lecturers and teachers, particularly Colin Fox, Daphne Matthews, Marjorie Morris, Roger Watkins, Brian Woolland and Brita Yates.

Anthologies involve tedious detail. Tamara Soom coped with permissions from poets, revisions and correspondence. This anthology has been greatly helped by lecturers and teachers, who over the years, organised seminars conducted by the Trust, enabling us to judge better the impact of poems on students of differing age groups and backgrounds. Dr Roderick Watt, Glasgow University, arranged not only the seminar but had poems of Sorley Maclean read in Gaelic by University staff, the first time many had heard the music of the poetry.

Roger Rothwell supplied the sketch from POW camp in the Far East; Michael Riviere the 'wanted' notice of escapers from Eichstatt.

Oasis and its Poetry

ı the Middle East in World War Two anything was possible. We were three
ıonths away from War Office in London (by troopship round the Cape) and it
ould be four years or more before we saw home. So in the Western Desert,
ıe 8th Army wrote its own rule book, improvised even its uniforms – if that is
ıe right word for the clothes worn by the officers in Jon's 'Two Types'
ırtoon below.

They read. They read books. No TV. No non-stop radio and cassette. Time
ı think. Penguin Books had begun in Britain a few years before, and for a few
ld pence one could buy reprints of the classics. The tanks going into Alamein
ere stocked with Penguin paperbacks to kill time in the waits between action.

Oasis, The Middle East Anthology of Poetry from the Forces could not have
een born elsewhere. Not for the first time did the Desert inspire thinkers and
oets. Above all, there was the Cairo base with its literary and artistic Services
lubs where we could go on leave. Cairo had publishers, too.

It was at 'Music for All' – the best coffee in Cairo – that three of us met a
ıonth after Alamein in 1942: David Burk, pre-war a journalist, Denis Saunders
om the South African Air Force and myself. I ran a tented Map Reading and
Javigation Instruction Unit in the Desert.

"My brother says he's on a lonely gunsite in Yorkshire—
two miles from the nearest pub!"

If Denis, who wrote poetry under the name of Almendro, had not been taking his latest volume of verse to a publisher that morning, *the* question which launched *Oasis* would not have been asked: simply, was poetry being written in this Second World War as it had been in the First? For if the question had not been put, and the decision taken to find and collect the poetry, this book would not be in schools today. There would have been no *Oasis*, which was published by The Salamander Society in Cairo. It appeared a year after we met, having selected from 3,000 poems sent by Army post from 800 would-be contributors.

Without that first anthology, The Salamander Oasis Trust would not have been established a generation later to rescue the neglected poetry of World War Two and eventually to produce four anthologies from 14,000 poems received. We knew the poetry was there. We, the members of the Trust, had all taken part in the original *Oasis* project as editors and poets. We had become all too aware, however, that publishers in post-war Britain showed little interest. Even recognised poets of the War were overlooked. The myth persisted that only the First War had produced poetry. The myth persisted notwithstanding evidence produced to the contrary and still persists even now!

In a decade the Trust has produced four anthologies comprising the two streams of Second World War Poetry:

a) The established poets, Keith Douglas, Sidney Keyes, Bernard Gutteridge, Alan Ross, G. S. Fraser, Hamish Henderson and others – poets who went to war and wrote;

b) More neglected and significant – for this was the real phenomenon of the Second World War – the unknowns, those who wrote poetry through the experience of going to war and wrote it for the first time. Some, such as J. E. Brookes, rank with the established poets, but all are vivid witnesses of war. They see, feel and record it all in literature's most dramatic form, the poem. Above all, their poems are history; the contemporary account.

In contrast to many anthologies, the *Oasis* series include only poems by those serving in World War Two and written at the time. This gives the poems their immediacy. Poems, especially from the unknowns, smell of war, an authenticity ensured by the compilers having also been participants in that War, both serving and writing. That is how it was. We were there. The poems above all, reflect the grass roots nature of World War Two. A literate and aware generation. Uncommercial. Caring, maybe innocent, an unwarlike generation that had to go to war. Hitler had to be stopped. A better world would come! A Churchillian belief, too: work for all, enhanced welfare and education, as in his speech 'A Four Year Plan' for post-war Britain, 21 March 1943. To the question, am I my brother's keeper, the answer was unequivocally 'YES'.

Victor Selwyn
Editor-in-Chief
The Salamander Oasis Trust

The Poetry of World War Two

'orld War Two has been called a People's War. It involved vast numbers of
·dinary men and women and their families, at home and overseas, in total war,
ɔt just a professional army fighting an enemy a long way away from Britain.
ɔr many of these men and women the war was to be the most intense
ːperience of their lives, and the horrors of destruction, separation from loved
ıes, and even the comic incidents they shared, turned thousands to writing
ɔetry, perhaps for the first and last time in their lives. Spike Milligan, serving
. the Royal Artillery in Italy, while helping to dig gun positions, heard a
milar noise nearby, but discovered that it was another regiment burying its
ːad. Ten days later, when German guns killed his own comrades and he found
ımself burying them, Spike was moved to write his first poem 'The Soldiers at
auro'.

Spike continued to write and make his name. Some of the poets of World
ʲar Two, such as Keith Douglas and Sidney Keyes, had already begun to make
reputation, but the great majority would have remained unknown but for the
ork of The Salamander Oasis Trust.

The poetry of World War One (1914–1918) had shown a remarkable change
om the feelings of romantic idealism which permeated the verse written at the
eginning of the war by poets like Rupert Brooke, to the feelings of disillusion
ıd anger expressed by Siegfried Sassoon, as the horrors of trench warfare and
ıassive casualties began to be realised. The final mood of such poets as Wilfred
ʲwen was one of deep hatred of the war and of deep pity for all its victims.

The poetry of World War Two is different. The servicemen and women of
ıe 1939–1945 War did not have the innocent patriotism of those who fought in
ıe earlier war. They knew that their own society had its faults, but they also
ıew that the German alternative was worse and that Hitler had to be stopped.
'hey knew that there would be few easy victories; they accepted the fact that a
ɔb had to be done. The common mood, therefore, was one of honesty and
ʲalism, determination and scepticism, allied with humour, rather than roman-
c heroism.

The poets of World War Two knew from the start that war was not glory,
ıd did not spend all their time denouncing it, although such poems as
Casualty' powerfully depict its horrors. Nor did they express a crude hatred
f the enemy, but often regarded him as a human being like themselves, caught
p in some great tragedy, and entitled, therefore, to compassion. Charles
IcCausland's 'Dead Japanese' is one of many poems which express this
ɪty, while Brian Gallie admires the courage of a German airman.

— 13 —

Distrusting political slogans about war, the poets tended to write not abou war itself, but about how their particular part in the war affected them a individuals. The strength of much World War Two poetry is not its epi accounts of campaigns or great battles, although there are poems about I Alamein and Cassino, but of smaller, more personalised episodes, such as Uy Krige's account of a machine-gun attack, 'The Taking of the Koppie', o Kenneth Wilson's story of the sinking of a U-boat. There are similar poem about other painful experiences of war, about a Spitfire dogfight, a patrol bein ambushed, a doctor meeting a victim from a concentration camp. The attentio to small details, the snippets of dialogue, the noise and movement in 'He Hamburg, Forty One', an account of a bombing raid over Germany, create feeling of immediacy, which is more than good journalism – they give the sme of war. The power behind these statements of personal dramas, told almost i close-up, radiate out to make clear the larger meaning of the war. The fiv wheat grains clutched by the prison-camp survivor in Phillip Whitfield's poen tell us more about the pity of war than many sermons:

> The moving skeleton
> had crippled hands,
> his skinny palms held secrets:
> when I undid the joints I found
> five wheat grains huddled there.
> In the faces of other people
> I witness my distress.

For many, of course, the war meant travel, not only to France, Germany an other European countries, but to Egypt and North Africa, India and the Fa East. Not surprisingly many poets responded keenly to these experiences, bu what gives many of these poems their power is not simply their capacity t describe new scenes, but the way the experience enabled the poet to explor wider feelings. Roy Fuller's service in West Africa led him to think about th differences and the similarities between African and English society, fo example.

What matters, Alun Lewis argued, are the particulars. Quoting from the Ol Testament Book of Job, he especially praised its description of specific wil animals. 'These are the particulars,' he said. 'The infinite of which I can neve be sure, is God the Maker. I prefer the ostrich's eggs warming in the sun. avoid speculation and haven't been touched by intuitions.' Some poets o World War Two, such as Henry Reed, were troubled by the fear of losing thei identity under the pressures of service life, and the passionate sense o separation from loved ones was also a recurring theme of the poetry. But sucl themes are often expressed, not through great abstract statements abou Liberty or Love, but through what at first seem rather low-key descriptions o the dull day-to-day events of service life, such as guard duty, learning drill waiting for letters from home. Poems about the boredom of war, those period hen nothing much seems to be happening and everyone is waiting for action, ften speak very movingly through small, but very precise descriptions of rger issues. Alan Ross's 'Mess Deck', with its description of off-duty sailors king it easy on board ship, writing their letters and even playing ludo, still rokes the shadow of death which menaces the whole peaceful scene.

Instead of writing about war in general, many poets wrote in order to try and escribe the conflict of emotions aroused by their experiences of living and metimes killing during the war. These are often reflective, meditative poems, metimes poems of conscience. Michael Armstrong wonders how the arm hich now innocently reaches for a book was able to kill so ruthlessly, and lary Harrison, who helped to make the small models which enabled air crews drop their bombs more accurately, asks how many people died because of e skill in her finger tips:

> Do you know what it is like to have death in your hands
> when you haven't a murderer's mind?
> Do you know how it feels when you could be the cause
> of a child being blind?
> How many people have died through me
> From the skill in my finger tips?
> For I fashion the clay and portray the landscape
> As the fliers are briefed for their trips.

World War Two came to rely on tanks, planes and all the products of odern technology far more than the 1914–1918 War, and this development is corded in such poems as E. F. Gosling's 'Mechanization' and Keith Douglas's Think I am Becoming a God'. While 'Mechanization' treats the subject ghtheartedly, Douglas's poem speaks of more than the change from horses to moured cars and tanks, and suggests that as cavalry regiments, with their me-honoured names of Hussars and Lancers, became armoured and tank giments, the social world where men rode to the hunt and point-to-points as beginning to change too. Although writers often admired the elegance and ficiency of much of the modern technology, the poets were always keenly vare of the killing power, as in 'Spitfire' by Norman G. Jones and Gavin wart's ironical poem 'The Bofors AA Gun'.

The war brought out a deep sense of comradeship amongst servicemen and omen. Because everyone was involved in the war, and living under the same reat, everyone shared feelings of comradeship and compassion for each other. his feeling is brought out in such battle-poems as 'Cassino' and the onymous 'Ballad of Anzio', while Jo Westren's 'Behind the Screens' reveals e unity between a caring nurse and a dying patient. 'Beach Burial' displays e same compassion and comradeship for all dead seamen, whether enemy or lies, for in the end the same sand joins them all together.

A great theme of the poetry is death. The poignancy of this theme was hanced by the fact that many serving men and women were in their twenties,

with their whole lives in front of them. Drummond Allison's poem 'Verity', fo
example, commemorates the death of a famous sportsman killed at the height c
his career. Many more poets write of the separation that death brings to lover
Olivia Fitzroy, a young woman serving in the WRNS, wrote movingly abou
her ever-present fears for her pilot boy friend in 'When He Is Flying', an
Douglas Street's 'Love Letters of the Dead', an insight into the workings c
Commando Intelligence, reminds us that dead Germans left loved ones behin
them too.

Of course, writers question the meaning of death and of so many deaths, bu
they find no easy answers. Although Frank Thompson's *'Polliciti Meliora'* see
death as some kind of sacrifice on behalf of future generations, and Sidne
Keyes' 'Advice for a Journey' anticipates battle in language which is almos
religious, others are less sure. Sorley MacLean, the Gaelic poet, can onl
speculate on why he was spared and six men were killed at his shoulder by
shell, while Dennis McHarrie's 'Luck' sums up the fatalistic approach to deat
felt by many serving men and women:

He died that's all. It was his unlucky night.

Not all the poetry is so sombre, and the war produced a number of poems i
lighter vein, such as the persistent grumbles about food in N. J. Trapnell
'Lament of a Desert Rat'. There are ironical poems, too, such as Douglas I
Vincent's comic complaint about flying and John Manifold's 'Ration Party
which points out the paradox of men working like slaves in the defence c
freedom from slavery. Most striking of all perhaps is 'Burial Party' by J. I
Brookes, a poem which describes one particular death in the terms of a blac
comedy.

Indeed the range and variety of the poetry introduced during and abou
World War Two is strikingly wider than that produced by the 1914–1918 Wa
It came from all ranks and classes, not just officers, and, while fully capable c
depicting the horrors of combat and brutal death, also produced poems abou
places, poems about the boredom and discomfort of war, and poems explorir
an individual response to the situation in which men and women foun
themselves.

Although many of the poets were not professional writers, they were ofte
well-read and extremely articulate. Paperback books and magazines wei
avidly read and passed round in the days before television, and the war poetr
exhibited a wide range of styles and techniques. Some of the verse is ver
formal, such as the regular sonnets of Jack Bevan and John Warry, and th
Housman-like lyrics of Michael Thwaites and J. B. Hilton. There are poen
written in the manner of popular ballad, too, perhaps influenced by th
soldier's friend Rudyard Kipling. There are narrative poems, poems makir
great use of dialogue, poems in blank verse, and even an imitation c
Tennyson's 'Morte d'Arthur'. But most of the poetry is written in the form c
modern verse developed by T. S. Eliot, W. H. Auden and Louis MacNeice i

he 1920s and 1930s, which is characterised by the use of everyday language, by
n ability to move from the serious to the ironical and back again, and by the
se of free rhythms and rhymes. Louis Challoner's poem about the Desert
War, Alun Lewis's 'All Day It Has Rained', and Peter Young's description of a
kirmish in Normandy, 'Recce in Bocage Country', all share some of these
ame qualities as poems. In Peter Young's poem the irregular lengths of the
ines and the stanzas, and the occasional use of rhyme, helps to create the sense
f the hesitant progress of the advancing force, and the use of such colloquial
vords as 'arse' and 'guts' adds a down-to-earth realism. But the poem describes
 tragic incident when an infantry platoon, which destroys an enemy post,
uffers heavy casualties itself, and the poem ends by speculating on the reasons
or the platoon's behaviour and the language used by soldiers to describe it.
Was it bravery or survival?

The poetry of World War Two merits reading because it speaks, often in
nemorable language, of what it was like to be involved in a great and tragic
var, and it speaks from a variety of points of view, from men and women, from
fficers and sergeants and privates, from almost all the countries of the
Commonwealth. Although the work of such poets as Keith Douglas and Alun
_ewis has been highly praised, the poetry of World War Two is especially
ttractive when it celebrates those reluctant warriors, the servicemen and
vomen who usually remain anonymous. Above all the poetry conveys the
eelings of men and women during the war more vividly and more precisely
han histories or newspapers or photographs. It has rightly been called the
utobiography of a generation.

Dennis Butts

*The poems in this anthology are arranged in sections which
cover roughly in chronological order the different phases and
the different areas of conflict, so that the book opens with
poems about the period of the 'Phoney War' from 1939–1940,
and concludes with a section 'Aftermath', with poems reflecting
on the end of the war and the return to civilian life. In addition
to poems grouped around phases or areas of the war, the
selection also contains poems on vital aspects of the war which
do not lend themselves to a chronological approach, such as
'The Home Front', 'War in the Air', 'War at Sea' and 'Behind
the Wire'.*

World War Two: A Summary

World War Two began in Poland in September 1939 and ended nearly six year
later in Japan, in August 1945. It began with Polish cavalry resisting Germar
tanks. It ended with the first use of the atomic bomb.

In its six years, World War Two spread through Europe, Africa, Asia, th
Pacific Ocean and Islands and the Atlantic. It thus became a more truly worl
war than its predecessor, the Great War of 1914–1918. It proved mor
destructive and involved the civilian populations far more. Historians estimat
over sixteen million military and twenty two million civilian deaths in Worl
War Two, mostly in Eastern Europe and the Soviet Union.

The Participants

The Allies: Great Britain and the British Commonwealth (Australia, Nev
Zealand, Canada, India, South Africa); France; the Soviet Union; the Unite
States, and to a lesser extent, China.
The Axis powers: Germany; Italy and Japan.

Origins

After World War One, the 1919 Treaty of Versailles sought to punish German
and re-draw the map of Europe, creating untenable frontiers, such as the Polisl
Corridor.

Reparations crippled Germany's economy. Amid widespread unemploy
ment the Nazi party were elected to power in 1933, supported by the Prussia
military, who had never accepted defeat in World War One. To them
Germany had been betrayed in 1918 by the collapse of the Home Front
Now glory would be restored. So Hitler tore up the Treaty of Versailles
ordered conscription, re-occupied the Rhineland and annexed Austria. A
Munich in September 1938 he cajoled Britain and France into demanding tha
Czechoslovakia hand over the Sudeten territory, its natural mountai
defences, to Germany and stand down its army. In return Hitler promise
peace and no more territorial demands. Six months later he seized the rest o
Czechoslovakia and threatened Poland.

Britain and France gave Poland a guarantee. To implement that guarante
they needed support from the Soviet Union, which had a common frontie
with Poland. The Poles, with their history and belief in their own powei

would have none of it, so frustrating any treaty. With war imminent, the Soviet Union opted out of a deal with the West and signed a non-aggression pact with Nazi Germany in August 1939. The pact had a hidden bonus for the Russians. They could recover territories lost after the 1914–1918 War: the Baltic States and part of Poland. In August 1939 the Soviet Union also had problems in the Far East, fighting a major land battle with the Japanese on the Mongolian frontier.

On 1 September 1939, Germany invaded Poland. Two days later under pressure from public concern – Hitler must be stopped – Britain and France declared war. For seven months the French merely defended the Maginot Line, the British Expeditionary Force defended North Eastern France, and Germany the Siegfried line. It was 'The Phoney War'.

Meanwhile the German Blitzkrieg crushed most Polish resistance in two weeks. Then on 17 September the Russians moved in to occupy Eastern Poland.

The Fall of France

The real war in the West began in April 1940, when the Germans invaded Denmark and Norway, countering Britain's ill-fated Narvik expedition.

On 10 May, the day Churchill replaced Chamberlain as Britain's Prime Minister, Germany invaded the Low Countries, then by-passed the Maginot Line to sweep the British Expeditionary Force to the sea. In ten days (from the end of May) over 380,000 troops were miraculously evacuated from Dunkirk – so many in small boats.

Italy declared war on the Allies. (In the run up to World War Two, the Italians had invaded Abyssinia in 1936.) The Germans entered Paris and France surrendered on 14 June.

The Battle of Britain and War in the Air

For a year Britain stood alone. German Armies occupied the countries across the Channel and North Sea.

Hitler needed command of the air to cross the Channel and invade Britain. In the summer and early autumn of 1940, in air battles over South East England, the RAF defeated the Luftwaffe. This, The Battle of Britain, stopped Hitler's planned invasion code-named 'Operation Sea-Lion'.

The Luftwaffe switched to the bombing of London and other cities, Coventry, Birmingham, Southampton. In turn the RAF bombed Berlin, Cologne, the Ruhr and communication centres. This became the pattern for five years with high civilian casualties on both sides. Later the Americans bombed Germany by day whilst in 1944/5 German day-time rockets, V1s (The Doodlebugs) and V2s hit London until their bases on the Continent were over-run.

The Middle East 1940–1943 and North Africa

In September 1940 Italian troops from Libya entered Egypt. So began the Desert War, which ebbed and flowed, attack and counter-attack – troops diverted to Greece and Crete, Tobruk changing hands several times until Montgomery finally halted Rommel's drive towards Alexandria at El Alamein in October 1942. The British 8th Army included Commonwealth Forces, from Australia, New Zealand, India, South Africa. This campaign proved the last Britain was to direct on its own.

Two weeks after El Alamein, American and British forces (British 1st Army) landed in North Africa. In difficult terrain, they advanced to Tunis to link up eventually with the 8th Army, which had advanced 1800 miles from El Alamein to end Axis resistance in Africa. They were now poised to cross to Sicily and Italy.

The Invasion of the Soviet Union

Notwithstanding a non-aggression pact, Nazi Germany invaded the Soviet Union on 22 June 1941. It proved a major miscalculation for Hitler and his General Staff.

So sure were they that a blitzkrieg would knock out the Red Army for all time that they did not even equip their troops with winter clothing. Instead, the German army was to suffer in sub-zero countryside outside Moscow and Leningrad for three winters. In the South they swept through the Ukraine, aiming for the Caucasus and oil. Here, Stalingrad on the River Volga became the key point. Whilst the defenders fought street by street, Russian armies in a pincer movement cut off the German 6th Army under Von Paulus, who surrendered on 2 February 1943, with a loss of 330,000 men killed and wounded.

It had a traumatic effect on the German Army. Stalingrad turned the war. From there, Russian armies moved across Eastern Europe until they took Berlin in May 1945. Russian military success cost them dear. A third of their land was devastated. Twenty million, military and civilian, were killed. Most German casualties in World War two were sustained on the Russian front, where they committed over 160 Divisions, two thirds of their entire army.

Italy

The Allies, comprising British, Commonwealth and American forces, captured Sicily in July 1943. When they landed in Salerno south of Naples, Italy surrendered. But German forces took over, leading to a war of attrition from Calabria in the South to the Po Valley and the Alps. Mountainous terrain and wide river crossings aided the defenders. The winters were cold and wet. The Allies were halted at Cassino which dominated the route to Rome. A diversionary landing was made at Anzio. Eventually, the Polish Corps of the

5th Army stormed Cassino on 18 May 1944, leading to the liberation of Rome on 5 June, the day before the 'D' Day landings in Normandy. It took another year before the German Army was finally forced to surrender in the north of Italy on 2 May 1945. The campaign tied down over twenty German divisions. Tito's partisans in Yugoslavia, in bloody guerrilla fighting, also held twenty German divisions.

Pearl Harbor: The United States and Japan

Japan began their war in 1931, when they landed on the Chinese mainland at Mukden. In 1939 they fought and lost a large scale battle with Soviet Forces at Nomandhum on the Mongolian frontier, their only reversal. For two years they waited, until on 7 December 1941, they struck the blow that brought the USA militarily into the War. (The USA was already involved in Lend-Lease help for Britain.) On a Sunday they attacked and severely damaged the American Sixth Fleet at Pearl Harbor, Hawaii. Within days Japanese planes had sunk the Royal Navy ships *Repulse* and *Prince of Wales* off the Malayan coast, to be followed by the capture of Hong Kong and the sweep through Malaya to take Singapore on 15 February 1942. As a result, many British and Commonwealth troops were to spend over three years in POW camps and work on the infamous railways in Burma, Siam and Sumatra.

'D' Day, Normandy to Germany

Under the supreme command of General Eisenhower, American, British, Canadian, French and Polish forces landed on the Normandy Coast on 6 June 1944. General Montgomery commanded the land troops. Altogether 39 divisions were involved in this largest sea-borne invasion of the War.

The British forces on the eastern flank encountered difficult, undulating country, lanes with high hedges, the Normandy 'bocage', where tanks grounded. On 9 July they took Caen. A month later they closed the gap on twelve German divisions at Falaise – another decisive action of the War.

Meanwhile, General Patton's American armour attacked south and west of St Lo, from where they swept through Central and Eastern France, whilst the British forces to the North liberated the Channel ports in a drive to the low countries, Belgium and Holland. On 25 August French forces entered Paris.

The drive into Germany suffered two setbacks. In September 1944, at Arnhem, the British 1st Airborne Division fought a ten day bloody battle. If they had succeeded the Rhine would have been crossed and the war ended sooner.

In December, the United States Army were counter-attacked by fifteen German divisions in the Ardennes – the Battle of the Bulge. Before the Germans were finally defeated they lost over 200,000 dead and prisoners; the Americans 40,000. It was the Nazis' last fling, though they continued to resist

as the Allies crossed the Rhine in March 1945. The Germans finally surrendered on 7 May 1945, a week after Hitler's suicide in his Berlin bunker.

South East Asia and the Pacific

The War continued in the Far East, where in 1942 Japanese infantry from
Burma had driven Allied forces back across the Indian frontier.

The Americans turned the tide in January 1943 at Guadalcanal. From there
under General McArthur, they began their Pacific island hopping, eventually
taking Okinawa, the Japanese base, in April 1945.

On the mainland, the British 14th Army under General Slim liberated
Burma, where Orde Wingate's Chindits raided behind Japanese lines in jungle
territory.

At sea, the United States first checked Japan in the Battle of Midway in June
1942, and finally destroyed Japanese power in the biggest naval action of the
War at Leyte Gulf, October 1944.

Two American atomic bombs ended the War: Hiroshima, 6 August.
Nagasaki, three days later. Japan surrendered on 14 August 1945.

Victor Selwyn

Dedication

Poetry belongs to us all. It is not the privilege of a group. We sing
poetry in our songs, recite poetry when we pray.

For poetry expresses our deepest thoughts and feelings. It is the
eye witness. From the waste of war it is treasure handed on by
young men and women, who wrote, to generations unseen. You!

— 1 —
From
1939
to
Dunkirk

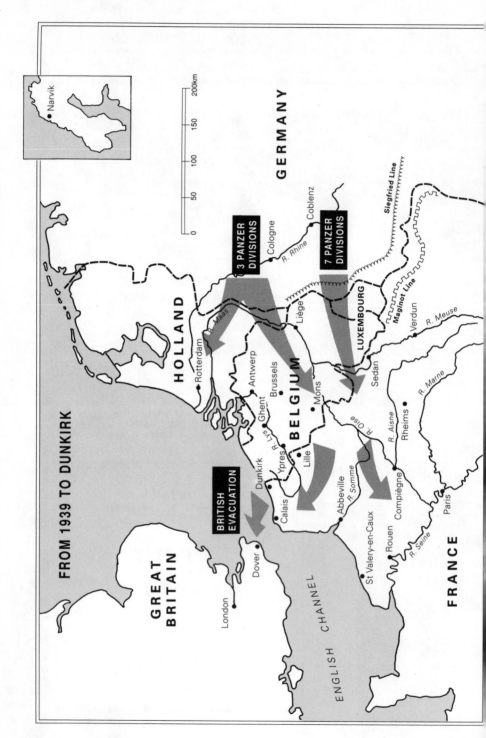

FROM 1939 TO DUNKIRK

GREAT BRITAIN

London

Dover

ENGLISH CHANNEL

Narvik

GERMANY

HOLLAND

Rotterdam

R. Maas

Antwerp

Brussels

Ghent

R. Lys

BELGIUM

Mons

Liège

LUXEMBOURG

Coblenz

Cologne

R. Rhine

3 PANZER DIVISIONS

7 PANZER DIVISIONS

Siegfried Line

Maginot Line

Verdun

R. Meuse

Sedan

R. Oise

R. Aisne

Rheims

R. Marne

BRITISH EVACUATION

Dunkirk

Calais

Ypres

Lille

Abbeville

R. Somme

St Valery-en-Caux

Rouen

Compiègne

R. Seine

Paris

FRANCE

0   50   100   150   200km

Even before the declaration of war in September 1939 regular soldiers were being recalled, and they trained the civilian recruits called up by age-group throughout the war. Initially this period was the time of the 'phoney war', when very little seemed to happen, and many of the poems deal with enlistment and training, such as Henry Reed's 'Naming of Parts', or separation and service boredom, such as Alun Lewis's 'All Day It Has Rained'. But this period ended in April 1940 when Germany invaded Norway and the Low Countries, and British forces had to be evacuated first from Narvik and then from Dunkirk.

— Epitaph on a New Army —

No drums they wished, whose thoughts were tied
To girls and jobs and mother,
Who rose and drilled and killed and died
Because they saw no other,
Who died without the hero's throb,
And if they trembled, hid it,
Who did not fancy much their job
But thought it best, and did it.

Michael Thwaites
November 1939

— Selection Board —

Three days of testing, observation and strain,
Why do we have it, what do we gain?
Interviewed here, cross-questioned there –
Did you answer correctly that questionnaire?
You think you did and yet daren't swear
That you're doing all right.
No – we're not quite
As bright
As we thought.
Matrices, curving with squiggles and dots,
Lecturettes, slides and group discussion.
'What's the difference 'twixt Nazi and Prussian?'
'What shall be done with the haves and have nots?'
That obstacle course to test our wits,
Should we wear denims or PT kits.
We jump from heights to show we've guts,
Unditch a car that's bogged in ruts.
Sergeants and Corporals, Gunners, too,
Mere numbers here,
trying to get through
And make the grade
Without the aid
Of an old school tie,
Strings pulled on the sly.
Who? Where? When? Why?
That's how it is, there's no omission
When the goal in view is the King's Commission.[1]

John S. Ingram
December 1942

[1] Conferring the rank of officer

— Lessons of the War (To Alan Michell) —

Vixi duellis nuper idoneus
Et militavi non sine gloria[1]

Naming of Parts

Today we have naming of parts. Yesterday,
We had daily cleaning. And to-morrow morning,
We shall have what to do after firing. But to-day,
To-day we have naming of parts. Japonica
Glistens like coral in all of the neighbouring gardens
    And today we have naming of parts.

This is the lower sling swivel. And this
Is the upper sling swivel, whose use you will see
When you are given your slings. And this is the piling swivel,
Which in your case you have not got. The branches
Hold in the gardens their silent, eloquent gestures,
    Which in our case we have not got.

This is the safety-catch, which is always released
With an easy flick of the thumb. And please do not let me
See anyone using his finger. You can do it quite easy
If you have any strength in your thumb. The blossoms
Are fragile and motionless, never letting anyone see
    Any of them using their finger.

And this you can see is the bolt. The purpose of this
Is to open the breech, as you see. We can slide it
Rapidly backwards and forwards; we call this
Easing the spring. And rapidly backwards and forwards
The early bees are assaulting and fumbling the flowers:
    They call it easing the Spring

They call it easing the Spring; it is perfectly easy
If you have any strength in your thumb: like the bolt,
And the breech, and the cocking-piece, and the point of
    balance,
Which in our case we have not got; and the almond-blossom
Silent in all of the gardens and the bees going backwards and
    forwards,
    For today we have naming of parts.   **Henry Reed**

[1] 'I lived fit for love's battles, and served not without glory.'
(Roman poet Horace)

— The Bofors AA Gun —

Such marvellous ways to kill a man!
An 'instrument of precision', a beauty,
The well-oiled shining marvel of our day
Points an accusing finger at the sky.
– But suddenly, traversing, elevating madly,
It plunges into action, more than eager
For the steel blood of those romantic birds
That threaten all the towns and roads.
O, that man's ingenuity, in this so subtle,
In such harmonious synchronization of parts,
Should against man be turned and he complaisant,
The pheasant-shooter be himself the pheasant!

Gavin Ewart

— Before the First Parachute Descent —

All my world has suddenly gone quiet
Like a railway carriage as it draws into a station;
Conversation fails, laughter dies,
And the turning of pages and the striking of matches cease.
All life is lapsed into nervous consciousness,
Frozen, like blades of grass in blocks of ice,
Except where one small persistent voice in the corner
Compares with the questioning silence –
With the situation of an electric present –
My self-opinions, pride and confidence of an untried past.

Richard Spender

— To Certain Ladies, On Going To The Wars —

Goodbye ladies, O ladies sweet, goodbye,
No more the gentle flowers,
Another life I'll try.
No more the scented evenings,
The tussles in the hay,
It's time that I was leaving
To live another way.

O, there'll be blood, my ladies
(And not all mine, I hope),
And damp beds under hedges
And washing without soap.
Black lice will bite the body
That knew your friendly limbs;
In barrack-blocks I'll envy
Your silken-sheeted rooms.

But goodbye ladies, O ladies don't complain,
It's time I learnt to shoot straight
Or fly an aeroplane.
So many lads I knew once
Are rotting under sods:
I owe them this one journey –
So farewell, pretty birds.

Henry Treece

— 29 —

— All Day It Has Rained —

All day it has rained, and we on the edge of the moors
Have sprawled in our bell-tents, moody and dull as boors,
Groundsheets and blankets spread on the muddy ground
And from the first grey wakening we have found
No refuge from the skirmishing fine rain
And the wind that made the canvas heave and flap
And the taut wet guy-ropes ravel out and snap.
All day the rain has glided, wave and mist and dream,
Drenching the gorse and heather, a gossamer stream
Too light to stir the acorns that suddenly
Snatched from their cups by the wild south-westerly
Pattered against the tent and our upturned dreaming faces.
And we stretched out, unbuttoning our braces,
Smoking a Woodbine, darning dirty socks,
Reading the Sunday papers – I saw a fox
And mentioned it in the note I scribbled home; –
And we talked of girls and dropping bombs on Rome,
And thought of the quiet dead and the loud celebrities
Exhorting us to slaughter, and the herded refugees;
– Yet thought softly, morosely of them, and as indifferently
As of ourselves or those whom we
For years have loved, and will again
Tomorrow maybe love; but now it is the rain
Possesses us entirely, the twilight and the rain.

And I can remember nothing dearer or more to my heart
Than the children I watched in the woods on Saturday
Shaking down burning chestnuts for the schoolyard's merry
    play,
Or the shaggy patient dog who followed me
By Sheet and Steep and up the wooded scree
To the Shoulder o' Mutton where Edward Thomas brooded
    long
On death and beauty – till a bullet stopped his song.[1]

Alun Lewis

[1] Alun Lewis greatly admired Edward Thomas, the poet killed in WWI, who had lived in Hampshire and often walked the Shoulder of Mutton Hill

— Sentry Duty —

His box is like a coffin, but erect,
the night is dull as death; he must not sleep,
but leans against the boards. The night winds creep
around his face, while the far stars reflect
the awful emptiness of heart and brain,
and trembling wires wail a requiem.
(If they were Sirens[1] he would follow them
to the sweet morgue, their magical domain.)

But no one passes; a stray cat cries out,
the moon emerges from a cloud's dark rim,
and vanishes; he walks, and turns about.

Next day no sad unrest bewilders him
who'd seen the planets fall into a trance,
the earth shed lustre and significance.

Michael Hamburger

Mythical creatures whose song lured seafarers to their doom

— The Tarn —

'We'd better split now. Keep behind the trees
Down to the tarn's edge. If there's a plane, come back
And meet me here: don't fire, they'll have MGs.
– We'll need to get as close as we can get.'
I heard the silky rustle of the skis
And stood stock-still, listening till it had gone.
I threaded one stick through the ring and strap
Of the other, and held them so in my left hand.
I cocked my tommy-gun – so loud, so loud
That little click! Zigzag from tree to tree,
Straining for any other sound beyond
The swishing of my skis, I ran to the tarn.
Between the black, still branches of a spruce
I looked across the ice: only the wind
Had made black random furrows in the snow.

John Buxton
Norway, April/May 1940

— Dunkirk (extract) —

All through the night, and in the next day's light
The endless columns came. Here was Defeat.
The men marched doggedly, and kept their arms,
But sleep weighed on their backs so that they reeled,
Staggering as they passed. Their force was spent.
Only, like old Horatius, each man saw
Far off his home, and seeing, plodded on.
At last they ceased. The sun shone down, and we
Were left to watch along a dusty road.

That night we blew our guns. We placed a shell
Fuze downwards in each muzzle. Then we put
Another in the breech, secured a wire
Fast to the firing lever, crouched, and pulled.
It sounded like a cry of agony,
The crash and clang of splitting, tempered steel.
Thus did our guns, our treasured colours, pass;
And we were left bewildered, weaponless,
And rose and marched, our faces to the sea.

We formed in line beside the water's edge.
The little waves made oddly home-like sounds,
Breaking in half-seen surf upon the strand.
The night was full of noise; the whistling thud
The shells made in the sand, and pattering stones;
The cries cut short, the shouts of units' names;
The crack of distant shots, and bren gun fire;
The sudden clattering crash of masonry.
Steadily, all the time, the marching tramp
Of feet passed by along the shell-torn road,
Under the growling thunder of the guns.

The major said 'The boats cannot get in,
'There is no depth of water. Follow me.'
And so we followed, wading in our ranks
Into the blackness of the sea. And there,
Lit by the burning oil across the swell,
We stood and waited for the unseen boats.

Oars in the darkness, rowlocks, shadowy shapes
Of boats that searched. We heard a seaman's hail.
Then we swam out, and struggled with our gear,

Clutching the looming gunwales. Strong hands pulled,
And we were in and heaving with the rest,
Until at last they turned. The dark oars dipped,
The laden craft crept slowly out to sea,
To where in silence lay the English ships.

B. G. Bonallack
May/June 1940

'*Nothing, I feel, could be more English than the Battle of Dunkirk, both in its beginning and its end, its folly and its grandeur.*'

J. B. Priestley's Postscript, *June 5th 1940*

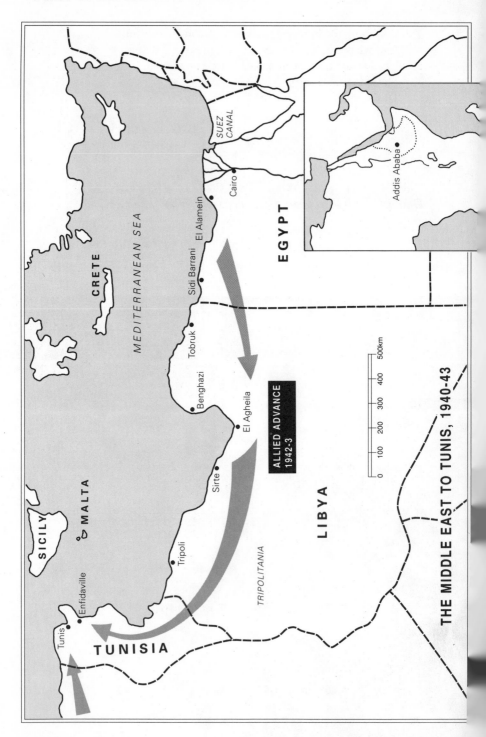

THE MIDDLE EAST TO TUNIS, 1940-43

— 2 —
The Middle East

The British and Commonwealth forces fought in the desert with artillery, tanks and infantry, but the desert also meant sand, flies, heat and daily water rations. Yet the conditions in the desert and the imminence of death also inspired poetry, from such men as Keith Douglas, who were already beginning to make reputations, and from previously unpublished poets, from the Commonwealth countries of Africa, Australia and New Zealand. Cairo became the centre for many writers. Some wrote about battles such as El Alamein or of the smaller conflicts, such as 'The Taking of the Koppie', and the poems express a range of emotions from the comic 'The Lament of a Desert Rat' to the pity of 'Elegy for an 88 Gunner'.

— Advice for a Journey —

The drums mutter for war, and soon we must begin
To seek the country where they say that joy
Springs flowerlike among the rocks, to win
The fabulous golden mountain of our peace.

O my friends, we are too young
To be explorers, have no skill nor compass,
Nor even that iron certitude which swung
Our fathers at their self-fulfilling North

So take no rations, remember not your homes –
Only the blind and stubborn hope to track
This wilderness. The thoughtful leave their bones
In windy foodless meadows of despair.

Never look back, nor too far forward search
For the white Everest of your desire;
The screes roll underfoot, and you will never reach
Those brittle peaks which only clouds may walk.

Others have come before you, and immortal
Live like reflections. Their still faces
Will give you courage to ignore the subtle
Sneer of the gentian and the ice-worn pebble.

The fifes cry death and the sharp winds call;
Set your face to the rock; go on, go out
Into the bad lands of battle, the cloud-wall
Of the future, my friends, and leave your fear.

Go forth, my friends, the raven is no sibyl
Break the clouds' anger with your unchanged faces.
You'll find, maybe, the dream under the hill –
But never Canaan, nor any golden mountain.

Sidney Keyes

— Beyond the Wire —

Beyond the wire
An awkward shadow dims the sand,
A twisted body,
Fallen with outstretched hand.

The last patrol
Returned, churning the night's quiet dust,
Leaving on the wire
A stain of blood to rust.

Six men went out
In search of new enemy mines;
Only five returned;
The sixth had found new lines.

As he crouched,
Dark in the pale light of the moon,
A sentry saw him,
Ready, alas, too soon.

The silent night
Leapt with the shock of rifle fire –
Now his body lies
Alone, beyond the wire.

John Cromer

— It's Always Mealtime —

Oh, they're queueing up for breakfast, they have rattled on the
    gong;
Hear the mess tins jingle-jangle. Let us go and join the throng.
There is porridge made from biscuits. There's soya for the fry.
There is tea that tastes of onions; there is bread that's rather
    dry;
And the cooks are looking browned off as they pass the grub
    along.
Oh, that look they get from cookhouses and drinking tea too
    strong.

Oh, it must be time for tiffin. What d'you think it is today?
Well, there's fish and meat and pickle mixed in some peculiar way.
There is yellow cheese as usual, and marg., and that's the lot –
Oh, help yourself to biscuits, 'cos the weather's ——— hot.
And the cooks are looking browned off as a dollop each one deals,
The look they get from arguing and never eating meals.

You can tell it's time for dinner by the fidgets in the queue.
And it's world-without-end bully meat mocked up as pie or stew,
And if you're mighty lucky, there'll be flour in the 'duff,'
But the chances are it's rice again, and rice is . . . rough.
So the cooks are looking browned off, slightly woebegone and
    worn,
The look that comes from cards all night, and lighting fires at
    dawn.

N. T. Morris

— Lament of a Desert Rat —

I've learnt to wash in petrol tins, and shave myself in tea
Whilst balancing the fragments of a mirror on my knee
I've learnt to dodge the eighty-eights, and flying lumps of lead
And to keep a foot of sand between a Stuka[1] and my head
I've learnt to keep my ration bag crammed full of buckshee food[2]
And to take my Army ration, and to pinch what else I could
I've learnt to cook my bully-beef with candle-ends and string
In an empty petrol can, or any other thing
I've learnt to use my jack-knife for anything I please
A bread-knife, or a chopper, or a prong for toasting cheese
I've learnt to gather souvenirs, that home I hoped to send
And hump them round for months and months, and dump them
    in the end
But one day when this blooming war is just a memory
I'll laugh at all these troubles, when I'm drifting o'er the sea
But until that longed-for day arrives, I'll have to be content
With bully-beef and rice and prunes, and sleeping in a tent.

N. J. Trapnell

[1] A German dive-bomber
[2] Free, surplus to requirements

— Mechanization —

Only seven months have passed but what a change they've made.
Remember how it used to be when troops got on parade?
'See those bits are fitted right!
See those girths are tight!
Mind you shake the blankets out before you put 'em on!'
How the nose-bands caught the light, how the steel-work shone!

All that's very different now. We dress like garage hands;
Gone now the clink of bit and spur; no trumpets now, no bands.
'Petrol, oil and water right?
All the wheel-nuts tight?
Did you check the levels up before you got aboard?'
No more, alas, the head-tossed foam, the fretful foot that pawed:
Oh glory that was Tetrarch's[1] might, oh drabness that is Ford!

E. F. Gosling

[1] A famous race-horse

— Night Preceding Battle —

Spoamy,
Slashing at the shore,
Salt skimmering in the moonlight,
And always that roar
Like a family quarrel. Tonight
I look across the disarranged sea,
Undulating unaltered, only I,
Different and detached, divining Me
Formulated as a breathing question-mark
Crivelling[1] in lust-pregnated casing,
Like bee seducing pollened virgin,
Questions 'Why?'

— 40 —

Why dust-born society advancing dust's decay,
Cradled in metal-moulded rhetoric, insane
Distortion of armed arbitration?
With this 'Why?' pounding, thumping in my brain
I demand God end His holiday
And influence the situation.

Yesterday I embraced my plough with masochistic pleasure,
Worrying if my economic seeds would be enough
To feed the hungry. Soil and work were the measure
Of my education.

Today I killed a man. God forgive me!
Tomorrow I shall sow another political corpse,
Or be dead myself. And strangely
I am satisfied to be applauded killer.
Holy Mary plead my dutied sin's legality.
Is there no end, reason, answer? Damn the sea!

Spoamy,
Slashing at the shore,
Salt skimmering in the moonlight,
And always that roar
Like a family quarrel. Tonight
They are rolling up the guns for tomorrow's battle.
I must not be late to hear Death rattle
In my enemy's throat.

The flame of Hell pythoning
Around my trigger finger insinuates coercion,
And feeling body's blooded-reeds contracting,
Dispose of humanity's humiliated feelings
And know that I am ready.

Christ, it's cold tonight!

Almendro

Waiting like yeast to ferment

— Christmas Letter Home —

To my sister in Aberdeen

Drifting and innocent and sad like snow,
Now memories tease me wherever I go.
And I think of the glitter of granite[1] and distances
And against the blue sky the lovely and bare trees,
And slippery pavements spangled with delight
Under the needles of a Winter's night,
And I remember the dances with scarf and cane,
Strolling home in the cold with the silly refrain
Of a tune by Cole Porter or Irving Berlin
Warming a naughty memory up like gin,
And Bunny and Stella and Joyce and Rosemary
Chattering on sofas or preparing tea,
With their delicate voices and their small white hands
This is the sorrow everyone understands.
More than Rostov's artillery[2], more than the planes
Skirting the cyclonic islands, this remains,
The little, lovely taste of youth we had;
The guns and not our silliness were mad.
All the unloved and ugly seeking power
Were mad, and not our trivial evening hour
Of swirling taffetas and muslin girls,
Oh, not their hands, their profiles or their curls,
Oh, not the evenings of coffee and sherry and snow,
Oh, not the music. Let us rise and go –
But then the months and oceans lie between,
And once again the dust of Spring, the green
Bright peaks of buds upon the poplar trees,
And summer's strawberries and autumn's ease,
And all the marble gestures of the dead,
Before my eyes caress again your head,
Your tiny strawberry mouth, your bell of hair,
Your blue eyes with their deep and shallow stare,
Before your hand upon my arm can still
The nerves that everything but home makes ill:
In this historic poster-world I move,
Noise, movement, emptiness, but never love.
Yet all this grief we had to have my dear,
And most who grieve have never known, I fear,
The lucky streak for which we die and live
And to the luckless must the lucky give
All trust, all energy, whatever lies

Under the anger of democracies:
Whatever strikes the towering torturer down,
Whatever can outface the bully's frown,
Talk to the stammerer, spare a cigarette
For tramps at midnight . . . oh, defend it yet!
Some Christmas I shall meet you. Oh and then
Though all the boys you used to like are men,
Though all my girls are married, though my verse
Has pretty steadily been growing worse,
We shall be happy; we shall smile and say,
'These years, it only seems like yesterday
I saw you sitting in that very chair.'
'You have not changed the way you do your hair.'
'These years were painful then?' 'I hardly know.
Something lies gently over them, like snow,
A sort of numbing white forgetfulness.'

And so good night, this Christmas, and God Bless!

G. S. Fraser

berdeen is sometimes called the 'granite city' because of its granite buildings.
ostov, a Russian city, the subject of German attacks during the war

— Ration Party —

Across the mud the line drags on and on;
Tread slithers, foothold fails, all ardours vanish,
Rain falls; the barking N.C.O.s admonish
The universe more than the lagging man.

Something like an infinity of men
Plods up the slope; the file will never finish,
For all their toil serves only to replenish
Stores for tomorrow's labours to begin.

Absurd to think that Liberty, the splendid
Nude of our dreams, the intercessory saint
For us to judgment, needs to be defended
By sick fatigue-men brimming with complaint
And misery, who bear till all is ended
Every imaginable pattern of constraint.

John Manifold

— Cairo Jag —

Shall I get drunk or cut myself a piece of cake,[1]
a pale Syrian with a few words of English
or the Turk who says she is a princess; she dances
by apparent levitation? Or Marcelle, Parisienne
always preoccupied with her dull dead lover:
she has all the photographs and his letters
tied in a bundle and stamped *Décédé*.
All this takes place in a stink of jasmin.

But there are the streets dedicated to sleep,
stenches and sour smells; the sour cries
do not disturb their application to slumber
all day, scattered on the pavements like rags,
afflicted with fatalism and hashish. The women
offering their children brown paper breasts
dry and twisted, elongated like Holbein's bone
    signature.[2]
All this dust and ordure, the stained white town
are something in accord with mundane conventions.
Marcelle drops her Gallicism and tragic air,
suddenly shrieks about the fare in Arabic
with the cabman; and links herself
with the somnambulist and the legless beggars.
It is all one, all as you have heard.

But by a day's travelling you reach a new world,
the vegetation is of iron.
Dead tanks and gun barrels split like celery
the metal brambles without flowers or berries;
and there are all sorts of manure, you can imagine
the dead themselves, their boots, clothes and possessions
clinging to the ground. A man with no head
has a packet of chocolate and a souvenir of Tripoli.

Keith Douglas

[1] Slang for 'find myself a woman'
[2] The elongated figure of a skull falls across Holbein's painting 'The Ambassadors'

— 'I Think I am Becoming a God' —

The noble horse with courage in his eye
clean in the bone, looks up at a shellburst.
Away fly the images of the shires
but he puts the pipe back in his mouth.

Peter was unfortunately killed by an 88:
it took his leg away – he died in the ambulance.
When I saw him crawling he said:
'It's most unfair – they've shot my foot off.'

How can I live among this gentle
obsolescent breed of heroes, and not weep?
Unicorns, almost,
for they are fading into two legends
in which their stupidity and chivalry
are celebrated. Each, fool and hero, will be an immortal.

These plains were their cricket pitch
and in the mountains the tremendous drop fences
brought down some of the runners. Here
under the stones and earth they dispose themselves
in famous attitudes of unconcern.

Keith Douglas
Enfidaville, Tunisia, 1943

— Elegy for an 88[1] Gunner —

Three weeks gone and the combatants gone,
returning over the nightmare ground
we found the place again and found
the soldier sprawling in the sun.

The frowning barrel of his gun
overshadows him. As we came on
that day, he hit my tank with one
like the entry of a demon.

And smiling in the gunpit spoil
is a picture of his girl
who has written: *Steffi, Vergissmeinicht.*[2]
in a copybook Gothic script.

We see him almost with content,
abased and seeming to have paid,
mocked by his durable equipment
that's hard and good when he's decayed.

But she would weep to see today
how on his skin the swart flies move,
the dust upon the paper eye
and the burst stomach like a cave.

For here the lover and the killer are mingled
who had one body and one heart;
and Death, who had the soldier singled
has done the lover mortal hurt.

Keith Douglas
Homs, Tripolitania, 1943

[1] A multi-purpose German gun
[2] 'Forget-me-not, Steffi.' (German)

About two hundred yards from the German derelicts, which were now furiously belching inky smoke, I looked down into the face of a man lying hunched up in a pit. His expression of agony seemed so acute and urgent, his stare so wild and despairing that for a moment I thought him alive. He was like a cleverly posed waxwork, for his position suggested a

paroxysm, an orgasm of pain. He seemed to move and writhe.
But he was stiff. The dust which powdered his face like an
actor's lay on his wide open eyes, whose stare held my gaze like
the Ancient Mariner's. He had tried to cover his wounds with
towels against the flies. His haversack lay open, from which he
had taken towels and dressings. His water-bottle lay tilted
with the cork out. Towels and haversack were dark with dried
blood, darker still with a great concourse of flies. This picture,
as they say, told a story. It filled me with useless pity.

from Alamein to Zem Zem *by* **Keith Douglas**

— Danse Grotesque —

The Devil played the drums when Peter died
An overture of bombs and crashing sound
    A whirling slip of splinter caught his side
    And deftly set his body spinning round

Alas! He missed his final curtain calls
A khaki Harlequin[1] in 'Danse Grotesque'
    With just a single vulture in the stalls
    To witness so superb an arabesque.[2]

John Rimington

A pantomime buffoon
A graceful ballet posture

— Latha Foghair —

'S mi air an t-slios ud
latha foghair,
na sligean a'sianail mu m' chluasan
agus sianar marbh ri mo ghualainn,
rag-mharbh – is reòta mur b'e'n teas –
mar gum b' ann a' fuireach ri fios.

Nuair thàinig an sgriach
a mach as a' ghréin,
á buille 's bualadh do-fhaicsinn,
leum an lasair agus streap an ceathach
agus bhàrc e gacha rathad:
dalladh nan sùl, sgoltadh claistinn.

'S 'na dhéidh, an sianar marbh,
fad an latha;
am miosg nan sligean 'san t-strannraich
anns a' mhadainn,
agus a rithist aig meadhon-latha
agus 'san fheasgar.

Ris a' ghréin 's i cho coma,
cho geal cràiteach;
air a' ghainmhich 's i cho tìorail
socair bàidheil;
agus fo reultan Africa,
's iad leugach àlainn.

Ghabh aon Taghadh iadsan
's cha d' ghabh e mise,
gun fhoighneachd dhinn
có b' fheàrr no bu mhiosa:
ar liom, cho diabhlaidh coma
ris na sligean.

Sianar marbh ri mo ghualainn
latha foghair.

Somhairle Macgill-eain
(Sorley Maclean)

— An Autumn Day —

On that slope
on an autumn day,
the shells soughing about my ears
and six dead men at my shoulder,
dead and stiff – and frozen were it not for the heat
as if they were waiting for a message.

When the screech came
out of the sun,
out of an invisible throbbing;
the flame leaped and the smoke climbed
and surged every way:
blinding of eyes, splitting of hearing.

And after it, the six men dead
the whole day:
among the shells snoring
in the morning,
and again at midday
and in the evening.

In the sun, which was so indifferent,
so white and painful;
on the sand which was so comfortable
easy and kindly;
and under the stars of Africa,
jewelled and beautiful.

One Election[1] took them
and did not take me,
without asking us
which was better or worse:
it seemed as devilishly indifferent
as the shells.

Six men dead at my shoulder
on an autumn day.

God's choosing some of his creatures in preference to others, according to the Calvinistic Church

— The Taking of the Koppie[1] —

No, it was only a touch of dysentery, he said. He was doing fine
    now thank you . . . What the hell were the chaps grousing
    about anyhow?
He was sitting on the edge of his hospital cot clad only in a
    slip with both his feet on the floor,
his strong young body straight and graceful as a tree, golden as
    any pomegranate but only firmer,
its smooth surface uncracked, gashed with no fissure by the
    burning blazing sun of war;
and with his muscles rippling lightly
like a vlei's shallows[2] by the reeds touched by the first breath
    of the wind of dawn,
as he swung his one leg over onto the other.

He was telling us about the death of the colonel and the major
whom all the men, especially the younger ones, worshipped.
'The colonel copped it from a stray bullet. It must have been a
    sniper . . .
just a neat little hole in the middle of his forehead, no bigger
    than a tickey[3], and he dropped dead in his tracks.
The major was leading us over some rough open ground between
    the gully and the far koppie
when a burst of machine gun bullets smacked from the kloof[4],
    tearing him open;
he was a long way ahead of us all and as he fell he shouted:
"Stop! Stay where you are! Don't come near me! Look out for
    those machine guns! There's one in the antheap and one on the
    ledge . . .
    Bring up the mortars! The rest take cover!"
Then he rolled over on his back, blood streaming all over his
    body, and with a dabble of blood on his lips he died – Christ,
    what a man he was!'

The boy reached for a match box, then lighting a cigarette, he
    continued:
'We came on them about ten minutes later, three Ities curled up
    on some straw in a sort of dugout
– as snug as a bug on a rug – and they were sleeping . . .
The two on the outside were young, I noticed. They were all
    unshaven. The bloke in the middle had a dirty grey stubble of
    beard – and that's all I noticed . . .'

As the boy stopped talking he moved, his hair falling in thick
  yellow curls over his forehead, his eyes.
And as I caught the soft gleam of blue behind the strands of gold
I was suddenly reminded of quiet pools of water after rain
among the golden gorse that mantle in early summer
the browning hills of Provence.

'Then I put my bayonet through each of them in turn, just in the
  right place, and they did not even grunt or murmur . . .'

There was no sadism in his voice, no savagery, no brutal pride
  or perverse eagerness to impress,
no joy, no exultation.
He spoke as if he were telling of a rugby match
in which he wasn't much interested
and in which he took no sides.

And as I look at his eyes again
I was struck with wonderment
at their bigness, their blueness, their clarity
and how young they were, how innocent.

Uys Krige
Addis Ababa, May 1941

[1] A small hill
[2] A hollow in which water collects
[3] A threepenny piece
[4] A valley

— Hospital Afternoon —

In the hand projecting from the blue pyjamas
The nerves dart like a pond of minnows,
Betraying a brief agitation in the brain,
Timid deer start in the parkland spinneys:
Through our shutters the fine sand blows like rain.
The waves of heat loll lazy aggression
Against our feverish island of illness,
The bumble buzz of an electric fan
Makes a weakly wind in a covey of coolness.
Whispering starts behind the crimson screen.
We lie out of sheets in defeatist languor.
The wardrobe mirror takes up my attention.
After lunch feelings grow fat in the head.
My nihilist brain nods its own suspension,
On a tide of treacle drifts off towards sleep.

Hamish Henderson

— Alternative —

The question rises almost daily
In the gunpit, grimly, gaily –
Is it the shelling you prefer
Or the bombing? – All the air
Crouching in silence, tensely waiting –
The distant thud – the deadly hating –
The whining scream – the crashing roar,
Forever nearer, – ever more
Intimately:

Then are the strong weak and the brave
Lie flattened low in their sandy grave,
Counting the leaden seconds dropping
Heavy as heart-beats, slowly – stopping –
Knowing each moment, dearer, clearer, –
Death creeps methodically nearer –

Or shall we stand, hands to our eyes
And watch the foeman in the skies,
Knowing the peril but unheeding
For the sheer beauty of the speeding
Planes that dive and, turning, mount again –
Light of their silver load – count again
The known numbers, note foreseen effect,
The chaos, sand and limestone wrecked
Into a halo round the sun
A cloud about our friendly gun?

I'd rather look death in the face
Born by a bomber's speed and grace –
Swinging down its rainbow arc
Like a falcon to its mark –
Than grovel like a nerveless slave
With nothing but his skin to save,
Crouching beneath the ugly Hell
Made by the calculated shell.

Louis Challoner

— El Alamein —

There are flowers now, they say, at Alamein;
Yes, flowers in the minefields now.
So those that come to view that vacant scene,
Where death remains and agony has been
Will find the lilies grow –
Flowers, and nothing that we know.

So they rang the bells for us and Alamein,
Bells which we could not hear.
And to those that heard the bells what could it mean,
The name of loss and pride, El Alamein?
– Not the murk and harm of war.
But their hope, their own warm prayer.

It will become a staid historic name,
That crazy sea of sand!
Like Troy or Agincourt its single fame
Will be the garland for our brow, our claim,
On us a fleck of glory to the end;
And there our dead will keep their holy ground.

But this is not the place that we recall,
The crowded desert crossed with foaming tracks,
The one blotched building, lacking half a wall,
The grey-faced men, sand-powdered over all;
The tanks, the guns, the trucks,
The black, dark-smoking wrecks.

So be it; none but us has known that land;
El Alamein will still be only ours
And those ten days of chaos in the sand.
Others will come who cannot understand,
Will halt beside the rusty minefield wires
and find there, flowers.

John Jarmain

*'Now this is not the end. It is not even the beginning of the
end. But it is, perhaps, the end of the beginning.'*
Winston Churchill, November 16th, 1942, on El Alamein

— Gunsong at Alamein —

Suns wheel in silence,
Dip and flatten on the desert's western rim.
Cassiopeia, the Great Bear and the dim Pole-star,
A huge and chimeless clock, turn our little time.
We are the subjects of the mad Khamsin[1],
Swept sandgrains eddied in the whirlwind
Passive as the old white snail-shells
Buried in sand that was limestone.

But also we impose our will:
In the cool morning the air vibrates,
Shells stream cleanly through the orchestrated air
As one by one
Our guns sing
In resilient steel baritone.

Charles McCausland
Egypt, 1942

[1] A hot desert wind

— Desert Conflict —

Cast your eyes and look over to the ocean and see ships.
It is far, you cannot see with your naked eyes.
Had it not been so, you could see the track of a big sea snake.
It is dusty, it is where the sea dogs play.
Raise the waves and hide yourselves, for you see the country
  has changed.
England and Berlin are in confliction.
It is where we saw bulls in a rage,
Each one being proud of its equipment.

A woman left the baby and ran away,
The women up north are crying,
They cry facing towards the east,
And say 'There our husbands have disappeared'.
Keep silent and listen to the war affairs.
Year before last in September,
There were great flashes towards the west.
It is there the enemy were troublesome.
The Resident Commissioner heard from home,
He heard about great deeds done by Africans,
He heard they were victorious.
Rommel neglected his duties.
The son of Makabo has taken part in those deeds.
The Chiefs at home heard – Chiefs Theko, Litingoana, Seele
  Tane and Mahabe

You always deceive us and say that
His Majesty King George VI is not seen.
A telegraphic message was sent from England to Tripoli.
It was received in the morning,
And delivered to the companies on Saturday, 21st June.
All Companies according to their race and colour
Coming to cheer the King.
There were those with three stars on their shoulder,
And those who had a crown in their hands.

The General Lyon[1] went down by the main road being silent.
There was wireless round his motor car,
And cannons guarding him on all sides;
Then the soldiers cheered the King as he passed and shouted
  HURRAH!

Calvin Makabo
Western Desert, 1943, on King George VI's ('General Lyon') visit

— Grave near Sirte[1] —

No poppies bleed above his blood.
His diary closed before last spring.
Upon his cross there greens no second bud.
He feels no more the sandstorm's sting.

The sweating dew upon his helmet's steel
Dries through each day to rust.
Caressing sand he cannot feel
Has blanketed his lust.

Eyes look no longer to the sea
His hope had often crossed.
Rocks shade his bones, and no dark tree,
No thaw for this death's frost.

Not British and not German now he's dead,
He breeds no grasses from his rot.
The coast road and the Arab pass his bed
And waste no musing on his lot.

D. M. Davin
December 1942

[1] On the coast of Libya

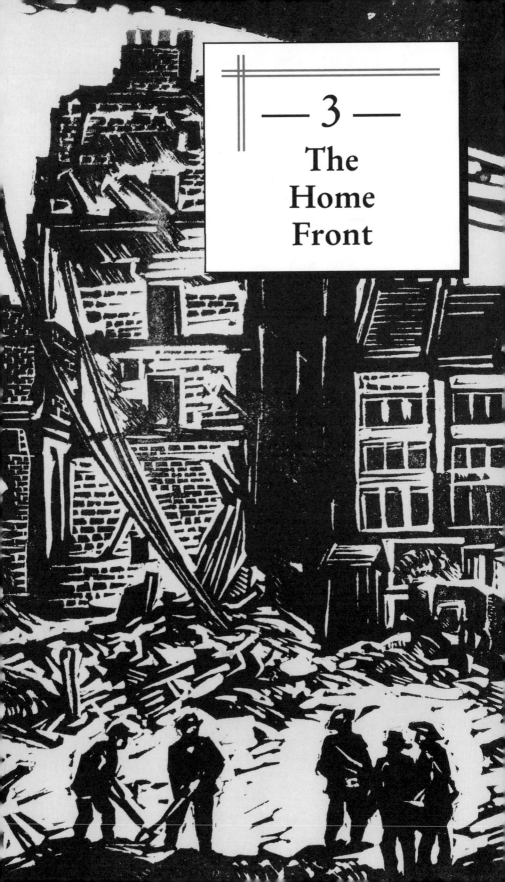

3

The Home Front

The bombing from the air sent people to the shelters at night; the daytime Doodlebugs came later. Housewives surrendered their pots and pans to be turned into war weapons, and many women served in home-based units, Joy Westren as a nurse, in the anti-aircraft battle against planes raiding South East England, and Joy Corfield and Grace Griffiths in radio and signals. And everywhere there were servicemen and women, training, travelling to join their units, sometimes thinking of civilian life and absent lovers, as in 'Night Piece for You' and 'Reveille – 1943'.

— Bombed City —

Walk with me to the silent city
walk with me in the fainting street
where the tramlines of evening
wind around the houses.

The churches lay the sorrow
of their bricks across the pavement
and houses no longer
cut the sky with swords.

Tendrils of silence
have bound the broken faces
the lens of day has caught
the overthrow of houses.

What fury here! what pain of living!
What monuments! what pitiless
enduring violin sounds
the white act of dying.

Woman lies with
city to her breast
crushed by the towers
and pain of mortar.

Child lies with
tourniquet of fear
and on his lips
the milk of death.

Inverted image of his city
reflected in the eye of man
his sorrow turns
and writhes like snakes.

Walk with me to the silent city
walk with me in the fainting street
let the knife of seeing
purify your strength.

Alan Rook

— Behind the Screens —

Meticulously
I dress your wound
knowing you cannot live.
In ten swift rivers
from my finger-tips
compassion runs
into your pale body
that is so hurt
it is no more
than the keeper
of your being.
Behind these screens,
soldier,
we two are steeped
in a peace deeper
than life gives,
you with closed eyes
and I moving quietly
as though you could wake,
all my senses aware
that your other self
is here,
waiting to begin
life without end.

Jo Westren

*'I think (the war) brought out things that I didn't even know,
feelings and abilities and depths that I didn't know I had. But
it also hurt me most terribly. There are things now that I can't
think about, and I can remember the patients. I can remember
which bed, what he was like, which ward . . . and also of course
out on the gun-sites I remember things when one was up
against the absolutely impossible, and somehow you'd got to do
it.'*

**Jo Westren, a nursing sister, attached to anti-aircraft
command in South-East England**

— Salvage Song (or: The Housewife's Dream) —

My saucepans have all been surrendered,
The teapot is gone from the hob,
The colander's leaving the cabbage
For a very much different job.
So now, when I hear on the wireless
Of Hurricanes showing their mettle,
I see, in a vision before me,
A Dornier[1] chased by my kettle.

Elsie Cawser

[1] German bomber-plane

*'Give us your aluminium and we will turn your pots and pans
into Spitfires and Hurricanes, Blenheims and Wellingtons.'*

Lord Beaverbrook's appeal to the women of Britain

— Morse Lesson —

A cold, cold room with cold, cold girls
In buttoned greatcoats, scarves and mitts;
Frozen fingers try to write
The letters for the dah-dah-dits.

'Faster, faster,' says the sergeant;
Slower, slower work our brains.
Feet are numb, our blood is frozen,
Every movement causing pains.

Yet – four of us swam in the sea
Just last week, on Christmas Day,
Through frosty foam and fringe of ice,
Warmer than we are today.

Joy Corfield
Isle of Man, 1945

— Steel Cathedrals —

It seems to me, I spend my life in stations.
Going, coming, standing, waiting.
Paddington, Darlington, Shrewsbury, York.
I know them all most bitterly.
Dawn stations, with a steel light, and waxen figures.
Dust, stone, and clanking sounds, hiss of weary steam.
Night stations, shaded light, fading pools of colour.
Shadows and the shuffling of a million feet.
Khaki, blue, and bulky kitbags, rifles gleaming dull.
Metal sound of army boots, and smoker's coughs.
Titter of harlots in their silver foxes.
Cases, casks, and coffins, clanging of the trolleys.
Tea urns tarnished, and the greasy white of cups.
Dry buns, Woodbines, Picture Post and Penguins;
and the blaze of magazines.
Grinding sound of trains, and rattle of the platform gates.
Running feet and sudden shouts, clink of glasses from the buffet.
Smell of drains, tar, fish and chips and sweaty scent, honk of
     taxis;
and the gleam of cigarettes.
Iron pillars, cupolas of glass, girders messed by pigeons;
the lazy singing of a drunk.
Sailors going to Chatham, soldiers going to Crewe.
Aching bulk of kit and packs, tin hats swinging.
The station clock with staggering hands and callous face,
says twenty-five-to-nine.
A cigarette, a cup of tea, a bun,
and my train goes at ten.

D. Van den Bogaerde
1943

— The Shelter (extract) —

In the air-raid shelter of the Underground
Stretched on the narrow wire racks ranged around
The walls, like corpses in a catacomb
With brows and cheeks cadaverous in the light,
By enemy raiders driven from hearth and home
War-weary workers slumber in the thick
Close atmosphere throughout the Summer night.
But, wakeful in the glitter of glazed white brick,
Dan sees a figure stumble down the stair,
A girl with wide eyes dazzled by the glare
Who pauses near the bottom; then with a moan
Sways helplessly, and, dropping like a stone,
Crumples up at the stairfoot. Hastily
The lad leaps down; then carefully makes his way
Among the sleepers huddled on the ground
To where she lies unconscious with still grey
Eyes staring. Stooping down, Dan hears a sound
Of heavy breathing; and, assured that she
Still lives, he seeks assistance speedily;
And skilfully the nurses bring her round;
When she sits up, bewildered, stroking back
The strands of chestnut hair from her white face.
Then, at a question where room can be found
To make a bed for her in that packed place,
The lad insists that she must have his rack.
So now he helps them as they carry her
And lay her on his berth; where presently,
After a puzzled glance at the unknown lad
Whose kind eyes look on her so anxiously,
Wrapt in Dan's overcoat she falls asleep,
Wornout by terror and shock, and does not stir;
In a fatigue-drugged slumber, dreamless and deep,
Recovering her vitality; while he
Against the rack leans resting, eager and glad
To think that he should have her in his care –
That he, among the sleepers who toss and groan
And mutter in their dreams, should watch alone
In sole charge of this slumbering unknown
Young creature come to him out of the night.

Wilfrid Gibson

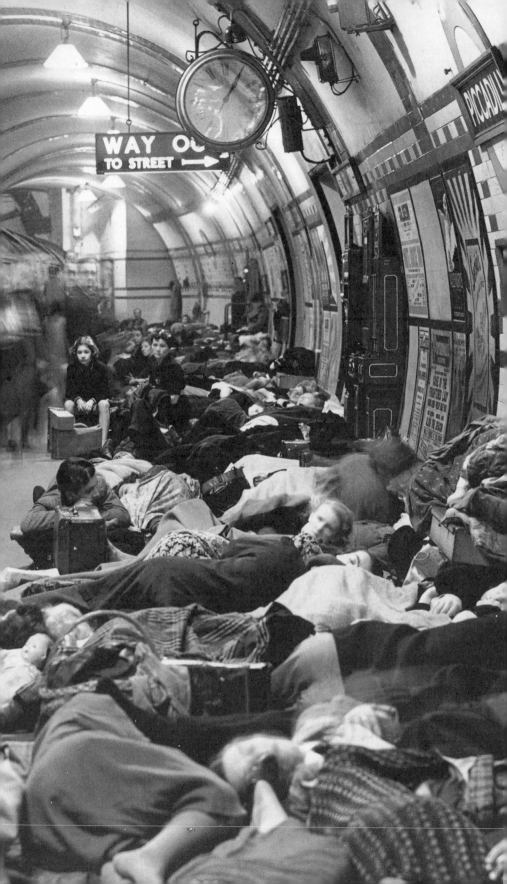

— Night Piece for You —

Smoke from the municipal dump blows sleepily over
Newmarket; racehorses on the Heath are ridden down
To breathy paddocks, and the last lights are all covered;
Evening, in Air Force blue, philanders at the end of the town.

Lovers in slacks and battledress on their physical errands
Loiter past, unfocus, sombre are no longer seen.
Thigh-deep already in shadow the cinemas stand
Dozing, and the dun staff cars, streaky as plasticine.

Far out along the sea-coloured coast of Norfolk,
Its cuts and estuaries, the searchlights stretch their arms
Palm uppermost, pressing up against the cloud-pack,
Strands of refusal combining in a shining skein to disarm,

Enclose or pierce or postpone that fierce image of ourselves
Armed in another sky. Sometimes, wincing like tracer,
I can glimpse crossing the space between two cloud-shelves
High up, the little involuntary movement of a meteor.

Two factory-chimneys a long way away fume and labour,
Their tops black against duck's-egg, their trunks in cinnamon.
A slow light, not of meteor, passes. Are our bombers
Loaded, as they tell us, with tolerance and the full moon?

As on the moors I am bitter again that we two
Only see the evening in ourselves, who watch the light
Weigh narrowly on living things, on cheek and tree,
And on this town, grey and riderless, now nodding goodnight.

Geoffrey Matthews
April 1941

— Reveille-1943 —

The day calls coldly, and the billet stirs
To habit-grafted routine; yawning men
Tousle their hair, stretching like sleepy curs
Roused by the boot of duty from their den
Of frowsy, warm and timeless luxury,
Sit up, light cigarettes, cough, and scratch,
Salvage their coin, and count their penury;
Or, rolling over, seek again to catch
The dim last moments of their morning dreams –
Of women fairer, kinder than they've known
In waking life; sun-splintered moorland streams,
And good brown ale in pewter, and the sown
And wrinkled ploughlands, cheeky music-halls,
Lampfall on cobbles and the peace that's found
With slippered ease among evening sound;
The candid noise of children laughing . . . to his own
Each dreamer would go back . . . go back. No good.
Boots clump on wood. A coarse roar batters on the hood
Of blankets, in mock rage; the squirrel cage
Of duty spins; day calls; and Now begins.

F. A. Horn

— Doodlebugs[1] —

A bomb, last night, fell close by Radlett.
The pulsing engine stopped right overhead.
Four minutes to the crash. Slowly we counted;
One girl cried 'Oh God! Dear God!'
The tension grew to bursting point; the blast
Shattered the windows. We breathed again.
Always the bombs come over in early evening
Just before we go on shift. We talk of rush-hour traffic
But underneath the fear remains. Death can come
From so many angles. Tomorrow, next week, next month
It may not pass us by.

Grace Griffiths
Shenley, Herts., 1944

[1] German flying bombs

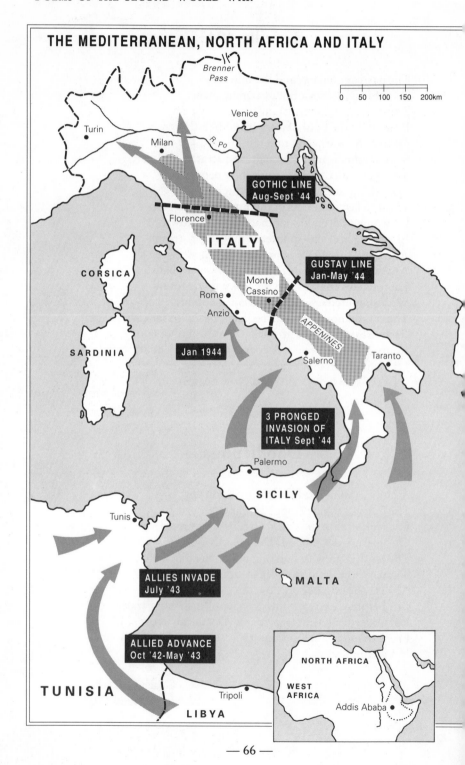

THE MEDITERRANEAN, NORTH AFRICA AND ITALY

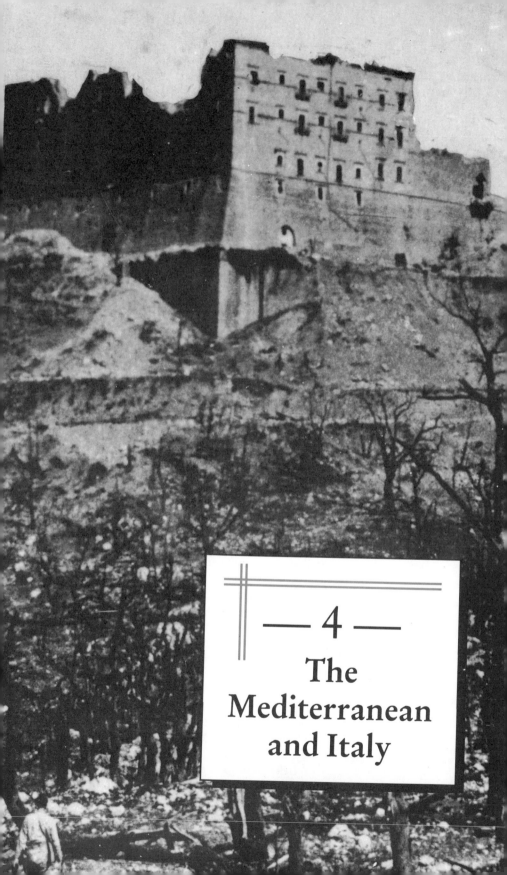

4

The Mediterranean and Italy

The British 8th Army from Egypt linked up with the 1st Army at Tunis, and went on to Sicily and Italy. Unlike the Desert campaign, the war was now fought in a country where civilians could be killed or made homeless, as 'Italian Road' shows. Les Cleveland described the battle of Cassino, and an anonymous ballad describes the bitter fighting at Anzio. Spike Milligan, an artilleryman, was moved to write his first serious poem by a burial party at Lauro, south of Cassino, and J. E. Brookes, an Australian infantryman, described an incident of black comedy. Erik de Mauny and Martin Southall recorded reflections after battles.

— This Italy —

I had not seen the earth so tender green
For two long dusty years:
Only I knew nostalgia too keen
Where sands of Egypt stretched
In utter desolation to the line
Of merging sand and sky. . . .
Until at length with bridled hopes we came
Upon this little land
So like the sea-girt shores of home it seemed
That head and heart and eyes had spanned
The continents between:
Not all a tourist's paradise man made –
Her tired cities knew
Such poverty and want and grim disease
The Nile is heir unto.
And yet there lay the land her soul had tilled
Throughout the stricken years –
The gnarled and roughened hands of peasant folk
Who understood not wars,
But from reluctant sod, with sweat and tears,
Coaxed the sour-wine grape,
And wove a patterned patchwork from the soil.

This, nature's garnering,
The iron rape of war cannot despoil.
The stalwart casas[1] and the ramparts lie
A helpless heap of rubble,
But still the twisted olive drops its fruit

Upon the terraced hill,
And calm, deep-barrelled oxen bear the yoke
Of wooden plough and mill.

Gwenyth Hayes

Italian houses

— Morning After Battle —

As if for a first time I have seen
The breathless outburst of this winter morning
And never before knew sun so tender in bare trees.
Nor, under the naked branches, green so green
As the silent fields. And the silence is
The calm of the late reprieve. We cannot bear
This silence speaking: so, as if ashamed
To show our joy, are wordless as we turn
Away from that country of fear no one has named.
There are birds singing in the crystal air.
We forget the fear that like a spider's web
Brushed at our faces through the lonely night;
Forget the pall of guns forever spreading
On cities, lights and perfumes, and release
The small history clenched in the fist of fear.

Mutter: 'They copped old Tom (or Dick, or Joe)
Sleeping – just there, look – under the wild hedgerow.
Wouldn't it make you . . .' Yes, when Death nudges,
'Old Flatnose', they are always ready to go,
With a brief sigh, like children woken from dream:
With simple words like these for epitaph
Masking the bright deep fury without a name.

Before these nameless faces what can be said
For a courage that braves the eternally private hell?
Yet it seemed like the promise wrought, the miracle sign
When a girl smiled, drawing water at the well.

Erik de Mauny
Italy, Winter 1944

— Ballad of Anzio —

When the M.G.s stop their chatter
And the cannons stop their roar
And you're back in dear old Blighty
In your favourite pub once more;
When the small talk is all over
And the war tales start to flow,
You can stop the lot by telling
Of the fight at Anzio.

Let them bum about the desert,
Let them talk about Dunkirk,
Let them brag about the jungles
Where the Japanese did lurk.
Let them boast about their campaign
And their medals till they're red:
You can put the lot to silence
When you mention – the beachhead.

You can tell of Anzio Archie
And the Factory, where the Huns
Used to ask us out to breakfast
As they rubbed against our guns.
You can talk of night patrolling
They know nothing of at home
And can tell them that you learned it
On the beachhead – south of Rome.

You can tell them how the Heinies[1]
Tried to break us with attacks,
Using tanks, bombs and flamethrowers
And how we flung them back.
You can tell them how we took it
And dished it out as well.
How we thought it was a picnic
And Tedeschi[2] thought it hell.

And when the tale is finished
And going time is near
Just fill your pipes again, lads,
And finish up your beer.
Then order up another pint
And drink before you go
To the boys that fought beside you
On the beach at Anzio.

Anonymous

[1] Germans
[2] Italian for 'the Germans'

— Counter-Battery Fire —

The sun is gone, the convent bells begin
their dolorous single ringing in the dales.
Subalterns flick their frequencies in gin
and gunners wash themselves in canvas pails.
The voices in the olive groves grow still;
silence and sadness with the dark descend,
drawing the moon up from the shadow hill
into a realm of stars that has no end.

Sleep folds us tranquil through the changing night
under the turning of the watchful Plough,
in army blankets, out of mind and sight.
The thinning darkness shatters. 'What's the row?'
'Getting it heavy over on the right'.
Telephone chinks: 'Bombard H.20. Now!'

J. Bevan

— Burial Party —

The stairs were shot away so someone fetched
a ladder, up we went and found him stretched
out on the balcony. His eyes were closed,
his face serene. You might have diagnosed
it simply as malingering except
that when we turned him over . . . thus we kept
him face up which enabled him to show
his medal ribbons to advantage. So
we took down the Italian flag that flew
forlornly from the flagstaff which we knew
would come in handy as his winding sheet
and tied the rope's end to his booted feet.
He offered no objections so we laid
him uncomplaining on the balustrade,
made a sign of the Cross to please the Pope,
prepared to take the strain upon the rope –
and pushed him off. The trouble was a ledge
projected from the cornice and its edge
lent him a foothold. Hanging by the toes
head down he must have looked like one of those
high-wire trapezists when we hold our breath
below while watching them perform their death
defying feats; indeed a passing troop
of soldiery had gathered in a group
to see the fun. However hard we tried
to work him off the ledge he just defied
the laws of gravity. We hauled him back
a little way and tried creating slack
by jerking hard but this brave officer,
completely 'hors de combat' as it were,
upstaged us and performed on it instead
a 'danse macabre' standing on his head,
and those below, accustomed to a much
more solemn undertaking, seeing such
an unexpected 'tour de force' appeared
to find it entertaining for they cheered
him to the echo. Then the flagstaff broke
and that was that. A funny sort of joke!
Our hero did not take a curtain call,
there was no safety-net to break his fall.
He caught his head a very nasty crack

on his parade ground like we'd dropped a sack
of water melons on it. Someone said
'That's cheating mate, he was already dead!'
War kills of course, but furthermore it warps
men's sense of humour – laughing at a corpse!

J. E. Brookes

— Morte d'Arthur[1] —

'So all day long the noise of battle roll'd
Among the mountains by the winter sea . . .'
And Arthur's forward section, man by man,
Had fallen in Tunisia about their Bren;
Smudged shadows lengthened out ahead of night
Emerging from behind the smoking crests;
And tired 'D' Company had lost its count
Of casualties. So, slowly, darkness came
And gave the heights to flames and tracer's sparks.
Alert patrols, wary of night-time's harms,
Crept out to kill the desperate, personal way.
Guns muttered distantly, guns unappeased.
Then grumbled Arthur as they tended him,
'These bastard legs have let me down at last!'
The gunfire answered him. And where his legs
Strong muscled, well reflexed, had been, a mash
Of splintered bone and blood-glued flesh was spread.
He spoke no more but took his time to die.
And Bill, his friend, picked up the photographs,
Threw two away, trampled and stained, and said
'I'll send these 'ome. Our Else'll want 'em back.'
Then orders came to make one more attack.

I. G. Fletcher

[1] The title of a poem, also in blank verse, by Tennyson about the death of the legendary King Arthur

— Cassino (Extract) —

At the face of the smoking crag
a horde of screeching machines
labour at this season's assignment:
spurts of furious dust rise and fall,
curtaining flesh ripped and thwacked
by fanged rods of shrapnel:
Engines howl full throttle
and claw at wreckage of sandbags,
smashed beams, spilled stone and lumbering
paraphernalia of heavy infantry
programmed for the intensive industry
of siege warfare in winter.
Steel tracks rage over pulverised streets
as enemy armour-piercing, self-propelled artillery
lashes pointblank at our newborn organism scuttling,
limbs entangled, heads devoutly flattened to earth,
huddling together under the barrage.
Each man clasps his blood brother
on that ancient rock of community
till every autonomous fibre is willed
into one prostrate, protesting entity
as the ponderous imperatives of shellfire

Signal that the position has been outflanked.
We, the living, hitch at weapons and scrabble
under cover of counter-battery fire
over mud-greased heaps of masonry
crusting the wrecked street and congealed
in frozen, formless landscapes against jammed
doorways and bomb-avalanched walls to the next
instalment of death shown the Via Casalina.
The dying wane with the expected stoic calm
Toward their silent territory;
They are already cast out.

Stay with the mob, you can't go wrong.

Now that soldier in the rubble
flinches, and instantly I feel
the thump of shrapnel pillaging
my temporary brother's flesh:
he cries out for help, and grips me

in a child-like hold;
I break his arms from their embrace,
and unbuckle his web gear,
open coat and tunic
and look where his blood
soaks into the dusty stones.
Kaput,[1] the stretcher bearers say,
Don't waste time on him: but I have to trace
the random processes of his death

I draw my knife and hack away the sodden cloth.
The carcase does not stir.

Flora of battlefields, discarded junk of casualties
strews the ground like trampled weeds:
I spread a dead paratrooper's camouflaged jacket
to cover both his stiff body
and the homelier shape sprawled underfoot . . .
The Spandau fire[2] from close range!
A sharp, bone-snapping shock
splinters the smoked-clogged air:
we run,
while I formulate the usual lies,
the righteous words to ease guilt
and sanctify the ritual death
of the man whose abandoned body
has been an expendable shield,
a viable husk in the ruthless cycle
of the omnipotent organism.
We run,
And awkwardly, gun at the ready,
I try to wipe from my shivery hands
The salutary, scab-like clots
Of the necessary victim's blood.'

Les Cleveland

[1] Smashed, finished (German)
[2] German machine-gun fire

— The Soldiers at Lauro —

Young are our dead
Like babies they lie
The wombs they blest once
Not healed dry
And yet – too soon
Into each space
A cold earth falls
On colder face.
Quite still they lie
These fresh-cut reeds
Clutched in earth
Like winter seeds
But they will not bloom
When called by spring
To burst with leaf
And blossoming
They sleep on
In silent dust
As crosses rot
And helmets rust.

Spike Milligan

It was January, 1944, Italy – a small group of Gunners had come forward to a small decimated wood outside the village of Lauro . . . We were to dig gun positions for our Battery to occupy for the forthcoming attack across the Garigliano river . . . I could hear digging – nearby – and thought it was a similar operation to ours . . . but the digging I could hear was a much grimmer affair. It was the London Scottish burying their dead – suddenly to the sound of the rain a lone piper struck up 'Over the Sea to Skye,' the words of the song came to mind 'Carry the boy who's born to be king' – it was a haunting experience. Then ten days later . . . came a midnight disaster – a German gun found our range and a direct hit on Sgt. Wilson's gun position – the camouflage net caught fire – the charges started to explode – all were killed or burnt to death except two. Next day we buried them – we had no piper – just the sounds of the guns around us – and I felt moved to write what was in fact my first poem.

Spike Milligan

— The White Conscript and the Black Conscript —

I do not understand
Your language, nor you mine.
If we communicate
It is hardly the word that matters or the sign,
But what I can divine.

Are they in London white
Or black? How do you know,
Not speaking my tongue, the names
Of our tribes? It could be as easily a blow
As a match you give me now.

Under this moon which the curdled
Clouds permit often to shine
I can see more than your round cap,
Your tallness, great eyes and your aquiline
Nose, and the skin, light, fine.

The British must be wicked:
They fight. I have been brought
From our wide pastures, from
The grave old rules of conduct I was taught:
Like a beast I have been caught.

If only I could tell you
That in my country there
Are millions as poor as you
And almost as unfree: if I could share
Our burdens of despair!

For I who seem so rich,
So free, so happy, am
Like you the most despised.
And I would not have had you come
As I most loath have come.

Among our tribe, like yours,
There are some bad, some good –
That is all I am able to say:
Because you would not believe me if I could
Tell you it is for you, the oppressed, the good
Only desire to die.

Roy Fuller
West Africa

— Italian Road —

Down the road they came,
The women of Italy.
The children, and the old,
Old men of memories.
Stumbling with their torn feet
On this broken road;
And we watched in silence
From the high turrets
Of our brutal armour.
Slowly they passed
Weary with children,
And the faltering footsteps of age.
Burdened with shock
And their pitiful bundles.
Treasured salvaged hopes
Of the home-makers.
These women of Italy
Powdered with dust,
Heavy with fear and fatigue
Trail past.
Only their eyes raised briefly
To the sun – and us,
From out of the sweat, mud and pain
Speak mutely, of the beauty,
The gentleness that must have been.
In them is no hate
Yet must we avert our gaze
Lest our pride be dry in our mouths
And the sweetness of our dreams
Be bloodied by their wounded feet.
And as they pass in the bitter dust
Of trucks and noise of distant guns
Our column moves
As the advance grinds on.
We leave them
These weary women of Italy
Lost in the harsh world of men
And our hearts grow a little tired
A little old.

R. M. Roberts

— Verity —

*n memory of Captain Hedley Verity, injured in Sicily. Taken P.O.W., buried
at Caserta. Pre-war, Yorkshire and England slow left arm bowler.*

The ruth and truth you taught have come full circle
On that fell island all whose history lies,
Far now from Bramhall Lane and far from Scarborough
You recollect how foolish are the wise.

On this great ground more marvellous than Lord's
– Time takes more spin than nineteen thirty four –
You face at last that vast that Bradman-shaming
Batsman whose cuts obey no natural law.

Run up again, as gravely smile as ever,
Veer without fear your left unlucky arm
In His so dark direction, but no length
However lovely can disturb the harm
That is His style, defer the winning drive
Or shake the crowd from their uproarious calm.

Drummond Allison

— May-1945 —

When we entered Venice it was flowers all the way
For the war was almost over, and we had won the day.

'Bellissimo Tenenti!'[1] cried the girls as I drove by
In my Regimental Splendour, waving beret to the sky.

We were wined and we were dined, for Tedesco[2] was no more
And everywhere we went, there were flowers on the floor.

But I knew beneath the flowers, so beautiful, so red,
We had ridden on a carpet of the bodies of the dead.

Martin Southall

'Most beautiful Lieutenant!' (Italian)
Italian for 'German'

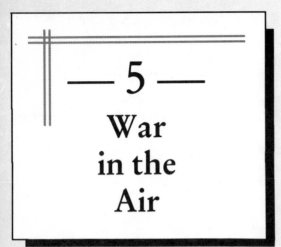

— 5 —
War
in the
Air

Fighters, mainly Spitfires and Hurricanes, courageously defended Britain from German bombers in fierce air-battles, particularly over Kent and South-East England. Our bombers wrought havoc on Germany, too, and 'Heil Hamburg, Forty One', 'Casualty' and 'Reported Missing', described some of their raids. But there was little Gung Ho patriotism, and Brian Gallie's poem pays tribute to a particularly brave German airman, whilst such poems as 'My Hands' and 'Luck' – regarded as *the* poem of the war by many who served – try to be absolutely honest and ask questions rather than ornament death.

— Spitfire —

Set upon a Kent hardstanding,
Nose up, knock kneed, neat and trim,
Eight oiled guns within the edges,
Lean and swift of limb.

One fine day a sneak air-raid,
Sirens screamed a sad alert,
From the blue skies bombs descended
Leaving death among the dirt.

Wheel and chock with my Red-leader,
Formed close by him as he soared,
Skidded to maintain position
While the Rolls-Royce engines roared.

With the gold of sun behind me,
Front a black Luftwaffe cross,
Coated bullet spitting at it
Saw the solid Stuka toss.

In the shambles lost Red-leader,
Received a stern command 'Return!',
Shocked I saw his aircraft halted
Watched the Spitty split and burn.

Below me I could see his victor,
Hidden face behind a mask,
My shots ripped a path across him
Then fire finished off the task.

Norman G. Jones

— To a German Airman —

Who flew slowly through the British Fleet

Perhaps you knew not what you did,
That what you did was good;
Perhaps the head I saw was dead,
Or blind with its own blood.

Perhaps the wings you thought you ruled,
With sky and sea beneath,
Beat once with love for God above –
And flew you to your death.

Perhaps: but I prefer to think
That something in you, friend,
No inch would give to land and live,
But conscious chose the end.

That something in you, like a bird,
Knowing no cage's bars,
Courage supreme – an instant dream
Of mind beneath the stars:

Misguided, arrogant, or proud,
But – beyond telling – great,
Made you defy our fire and fly
Straight on, to meet your fate.

Steel-capped, we cowered as you went,
Defiant and alone;
A noble thing, we watched you wing
Your way to the unknown.

You passed us, still a mile from death,
Rocked by the wind of shell;
We held our breath, until to death
Magnificent you fell.

Whatever comet lit your track –
Contempt, belief, or hate –
You let us see an enemy
Deliberately great.

Brian Gallie

— Heil Hamburg, Forty One —

Our height is just ten thousand feet. The night,
though dimly lit by stars, is solemn, quiet, still.
My sergeant in the nose, his target map a sorry, crumpled mess,
His bombsight checked, his figures proved and double proved,
I sniff. The smell of fear is in this craft, it clings.
We wait the tracking guns below to find us.

Now into the glare – ahead the searchlights probe, then group,
And in their mingling hold a victim, fluttering moth,
The guns are on him now: we watch the killing
In that bright slaughterhouse where we shall be
Two minutes hence. I check the time and wait.
And there he goes! He burns, he falls, he spins,
And still he drops, and still we look and pray for 'chutes –
But no, he's gone. There will be no prisoners to feed.
God rest them all. And now . . . it's our stint in the crucible:
We start survival drill. I turn full five to starboard,
Two hundred up, then port for ten. Down again, five more,
No constant course to aid the murd'rous guns below,
No rest, no peace, no hiding place, naught but human skill our
   aid.
And then the last of it – and us? – the straight run in on target.
The hoarse non-actor's voice from nose and lung and heart –
'Bombs gone'. Lightened, the aircraft leaps, I turn then,
Diving to port, a vertical steep turn. We enter cloud, glad
   shelter,
A thund'rous crack, blue flames along the wing-edge, we drop,
   rise.
The static deafens: my cockney aimer drives away my terror
'Cumulus, skipper, currents vertical, course two seventy for
   home'
Home . . . happy word, land we left three hours since.

While in Hamburg they rake the cinders of the dead from one
   small plane.

Redmond Macdonogh
In a Bristol Blenheim, Autumn 1941

— My Hands —

Do you know what it is like to have death in your hands
when you haven't a murderer's mind?
Do you know how it feels when you could be the cause
of a child being blind?
How many people have died through me
From the skill in my finger tips?
For I fashion the clay and portray the landscape
As the fliers are briefed for their trips

Do those young men in blue feel as I do
The destruction
The pain.
Let me cover my eyes as you cover the skies
Let me pray it can't happen again.
Don't show me the pictures you take as you fly,
They're ruins and scape – little more.

Is all this part
Of the madness we choose to call War?
If there is a God up above who listens at all
Does he know why this has to be.
Did he give me my hands just to fashion the plans
That my own land may always be free?

Mary E. Harrison

Mary E. Harrison, topographical model maker in the WAAF making models to brief air crews for bombing raids, wrote the poem after being shown the photographs taken after a raid and then remembering the photographs from which she had worked.

— Casualty —

'Easy boys; leave it to the doc . . .'
'Afraid he's pretty bad, doc; we've not heard
A word from him since just before we bombed . . .'
Hands under his arms and knees
Lift him down gently; unplug his intercomm.
And disconnect his oxygen.
Now guide his shoulders and dislodge his feet
From the wrecked turret;
So lay him down, and look at him.

'Much you can do?'
    'No – I'm afraid he's dead,
Has been for hours –' 'Oh. Well, I'm sorry –'
                        'Yes,
Probably never knew what hit him.'
But in the torchlight you can see
His face is frozen:
Cannon shells pumped into his side
From neck to knee. Skin white like rigid lard,
Eyes glazed, with frosted lashes,
Flying suit crusted with red chalk
That was his blood . . .
                Such is the cold
In a smashed turret open to the wind
Torn at that height and speed through icy darkness.
Yesterday
I heard someone complain
'Last night the bombers in procession
Kept me awake . . .'

David Stafford Clark
March 1944

— Death of a Man of Kent —

Now he could see the fields that lay below,
The tiny chequered towns, the London train
Just steaming into Canterbury with slow
And sinuous movement. Then the steel rain
Of bullet after bullet seemed to tear
His Hurricane in pieces. As he fell
He thought he heard come to his dying ear
Church bells from Wingham tolling out his knell.

The land he loved stretched out her arms to meet him,
The land he'd sought to save now called him home;
The smiling fields of Kent were there to greet him,
And to his graveside all his neighbours come;
Men with bowed heads, and girls dissolved in tears,
As if he'd died in bed and full of years.

J. M. Collard

— Reported Missing —

With broken wing they limped across the sky
caught in late sunlight, with their gunner dead,
one engine gone, – the type was out-of-date, –
blood on the fuselage turning brown from red:

knew it was finished, looking at the sea
which shone back patterns in kaleidoscope
knew that their shadow would meet them by the way,
close and catch at them, drown their single hope:

sat in this tattered scarecrow of the sky
hearing it cough, the great plane catching
now the first dark clouds upon her wing-base, –
patching the great tear in evening mockery.

So two men waited, saw the third dead face,
and wondered when the wind would let them die.

John Bayliss

— Silly Sort of Past-Time —

It's a silly sort of past-time
As a wise old bird once said
To spend the whole night flying
Whilst others are in bed.

You spend four hours looking
For a pin-point on the ground
But no-one wants to see you
When the object has been found.

They only show displeasure
When you spoil their forty winks
So they throw the whole lot at you
Which includes the kitchen sink.

Then, if you're really lucky
And you've not come out the worst
You spend four hours looking
For the place you came from, first.

Donald E. Vincent

*He was well below me now. I could see him clearly by
squinting down out of my cockpit. He wasn't diving and he
wasn't spinning either. He was turning slowly over and over
like a leaf, the black smoke pouring out from the starboard
engine. Then I saw one . . . two . . . three people jump out of
the fuselage and go tumbling earthwards with legs and arms
outstretched in grotesque attitudes, and a moment later one . . .
two . . . three parachutes billowed open and began floating
gently down between the cliffs towards the narrow valley
below.*

**Roald Dahl, on shooting down a German bomber over Greece
From his autobiography** Going Solo

— When He Is Flying —

When I was young I thought that if Death came
He would come suddenly, and with a swift hand kill,
Taking all feeling;
Want, laughter and fear;
Leaving a cold and soulless shell on earth
While the small winged soul
Flew on,
At peace.
I used to think those things when I was young,
But now I know.
I know
Death stands beside me, never very far,
An unseen shadow, just beyond my view
And if I hear an engine throb and fade
Or see a neat formation pass
Or a lone fighter soar, hover and dart,
He takes another step more near
And lays his cold unhurried hand on my heart.

Olivia Fitzroy

Olivia's pilot boy-friend was killed at Singapore in 1945.

— Luck —

I suppose they'll say his last thoughts were of simple things,
Of April back at home, and the late sun on his wings;
Or that he murmured someone's name
As earth reclaimed him sheathed in flame.
Oh God! Let's have no more of empty words,
Lip service ornamenting death!
The worms don't spare the hero;
Nor can children feed upon resounding praises of his deed.
'He died who loved to live,' they'll say,
'Unselfishly so we might have today!'
Like hell! He fought because he had to fight;
He died that's all. It was his unlucky night.

Dennis McHarrie

— Combat Report —

'Just then I saw the bloody Hun'
You saw the Hun? You, light and easy,
Carving the soundless daylight. 'I was breezy
When I saw that Hun.' Oh wonder
Pattern of stress, of nerve poise, flyer,
Overtaking time. 'He came out under
Nine-tenths cloud, but I was higher.'
Did Michelangelo aspire,
Painting the laughing cumulus, to ride
The majesty of air. 'He was a trier
I'll give him that, the Hun.' So you convert
Ultimate sky to air speed, drift and cover;
Sure with the tricky tools of God and lover.
'I let him have a sharp four-second squirt,
Closing to fifty yards. He went on fire.'
Your deadly petals painted, you exert
A simple stature. Man-high, without pride,
You pick your way through heaven and the dirt.
'He burnt out in the air; that's how the poor sod died.'

John Pudney

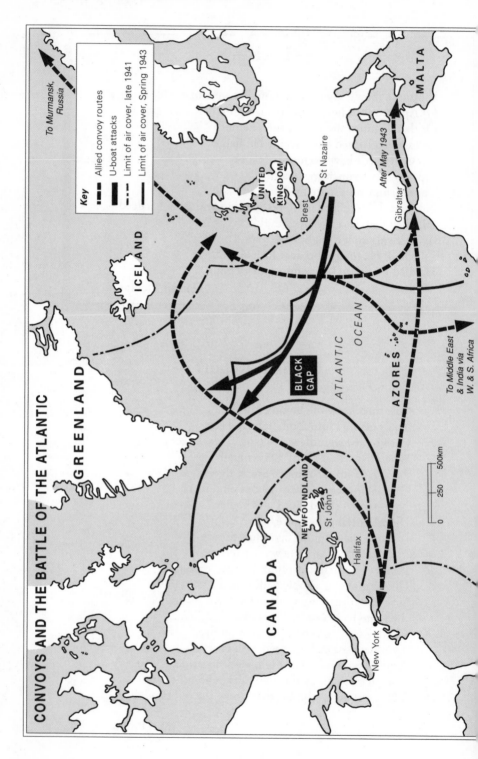

CONVOYS AND THE BATTLE OF THE ATLANTIC

Key
Allied convoy routes
U-boat attacks
Limit of air cover, late 1941
Limit of air cover, Spring 1943

To Murmansk, Russia

MALTA

After May 1943

St Nazaire

UNITED KINGDOM

Brest

Gibraltar

ICELAND

ATLANTIC OCEAN

GREENLAND

BLACK GAP

AZORES

To Middle East & India via W. & S. Africa

NEWFOUNDLAND

St John

CANADA

Halifax

New York

0 250 500km

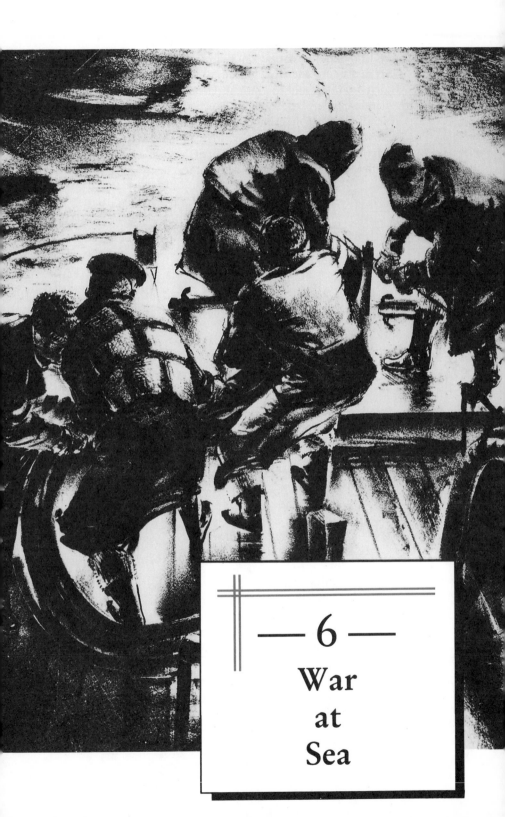

—6—

War
at
Sea

Naval operations centred on guarding the supply routes from the USA to Britain, and from Britain to Russia, which were vulnerable to dive bombers and to German U-boats. Kenneth Wilson's poem 'Atlantic Convoy' enacts such a journey, while Norman Hampson's 'Assault Convoy' describes a convoy carrying men for a landing on enemy soil. Other poems by Roy Fuller, Alan Ross and John Wedge evoke the boredom and anxieties while waiting for action, and 'Beach Burial' laments the fate of too many mariners.

— Atlantic Convoy —

Zig. . . .
    Zag. . . .
Zig. . . .
    Zag. . . .
Zig to port;
    Zag to starboard;
Follow the wake of the ship ahead.
Zig. . . .
    Zag. . . .
All peaceful men should be in bed.
Zig. . . .
    Zag. . . .
Phosphorus gleams upon the water,
A ghostly light inviting slaughter.
Zig. . . .
    Zag. . . .
Pin-n-n-n-n-g. Pin-n-n-n-n-g.
No echo from the Asdic dome[1]
within the arc it has to roam.
Pin-n-n-n-g. Pin-n-n-n-n-g.
Thrump! Thrump! Thrump! Thrump!
The twisting, churning of the screw
drowning the talk from 'B' gun's crew.
Thrump! Thrump! Thrump! Thrump!
The watch has two more hours to go.
Zig. . . .
Zag. . . .
The time crawls on, so slow, so slow.
Pin-n-n-n-n-g. Pin-n-n-n-n-g.
Tired eyes straining without hope
of ever sighting a periscope.

Two more hours, then to my bunk –
Providing we have not been sunk!
    Thrump! Thrump!
    Pin-n-n-n-n-g. Pin-n-n-n-n-g.
    Zig. . . .
        Zag. . . .
Nothing yet to be seen
upon the moving radar screen.
Thrump! Thrump!
The night is cold with signs of snow.
Smells permeate from the decks below.

PING! PING! PING! PING!

Contact . . . contact. . . .
Range and bearing. . . .

ACTION STATIONS!

Men tumble from their hammocks swearing.
Short sharp rings on the alarm bell.

'A' GUN LOAD WITH STAR SHELL.

A tiny dot on the radar screen:
a U-boat on the surface?
    Crash-dived . . . now no longer seen.

INCREASE SPEED TO TWENTY KNOTS.

Thrump! Thrump! Thrump! Thrump!
Ping! Ping! Ping! Ping!
Range closing.
Bows nosing.
Closing fast.
Shadowy vessels streaming past.

Ping! Ping! Ping! Ping!

SET THE CHARGES!

    The pinging stops. . . .
Target right below.
Press hard the knob.

Depth-charges go. . . .
    Boom-m-m-m-m
        Boom-m-m-m-m
            Boom-m-m-m-m
                Boom-m-m-m-m

Dropped astern, thrown to each quarter;
brilliant flashes on the water;
flashes making night like day,
decks awash with falling spray.

Turn through an arc of one-eight-o
over the spot where down below
men are dying.

Silence.

Then crunch . . . crunch . . . crunch upon the hydrophone.[2]
She's breaking up down there alone.
The reek of oil invades the night.

STOP ENGINES! BURN A SEARCHLIGHT!

Some tangled wreckage, a leg or two:
of oily corpses there's a few;
enough evidence of a kill.
So this night's score is now one-nil!

Thrump! Thrump! Thrump! Thrump!

Back on station.

SLOW AHEAD!

And in Greenhow they're still abed.

Pin-n-n-n-g. Pin-n-n-n-g.
Zig. . . .
        Zag. . . .
Leave the bloated bodies torn.
It's lighter now, here comes the dawn,
morning for us, who have come through,
but never again for the U-boat's crew.
Yet in killing I find no delight;
perhaps I'll be dead before tonight.

            Zig. . . .
        Zag. . . .
            Zig. . . .
        Zag. . . .

Kenneth Wilson
Written in HMS Bideford, August 1941

[1] A device to detect U-boats
[2] A listening device

— Mess Deck —

The bulkhead sweating, and under naked bulbs
Men writing letters, playing Ludo. The light
Cuts their arms off at the wrist, only the dice
Lives. Hammocks swing, nuzzling-in tight
Like foals into flanks of mares. Bare shoulders
Glisten with oil, tattoo-marks rippling their scales on
Mermaids or girls' thighs as dice are shaken, cards played.
We reach for sleep like a gas, randy for oblivion.
But, laid out on lockers, some get waylaid;
And lie stiff, running off films in the mind's dark-room.
The air soupy, yet still cold; a beam sea rattles
Cups smelling of stale tea, knocks over a broom.
The light is watery, like the light of the sea-bed;
Marooned in it, stealthy as fishes, we may even be dead.

Alan Ross

On deck you slept in a hammock, on the mess table, or on the floor.
Those prone to sea-sickness were encouraged by others to choose the
floor.

B. W. Brown

— Royal Naval Air Station —

The piano, hollow and sentimental, plays,
And outside, falling in a moonlit haze,
The rain is endless as the empty days.

Here in the mess, on beds, on benches, fall
The blue serge limbs in shapes fantastical:
The photographs of girls are on the wall.

And the songs of the minute walk into our ears;
Behind the easy words are difficult tears:
The pain which stabs is dragged out over years.

A ghost has made uneasy every bed.
You are not you without me and *The dead
Only are pleased to be alone* it said.

And hearing it silently the living cry
To be again themselves, or sleeping try
To dream it is impossible to die.

Roy Fuller

— Still No Letter ... —

There's still no letter ...
                In my troubled mind
I seek a reason, and quickly reasons find,
Indeed they tumble in, to be discarded
Each as it comes ... It could be that
You're very busy; missed the evening post;
Or else it's held up in the mail. A host
Of explanations ... Yet that gnawing fear
O'errides them, still keeps dunning at me that
You just don't want to write. And vainly I
Attempt to thrust aside the thought; deny
It with your last note, and the one before.
But no. I must resign myself to wait

Until tomorrow, or the next day and
A day. Surely then I see your hand-
Writing and envelope. And life is sweet, until
A week or so, when . . .
                    Still no letter.

John Wedge

— Coming into the Clyde —

Part of me for ever is the January morning
Coming into the Clyde in the frosty moonlight
And the land under snow and the snow under moonlight,
Fall upon fall, a soundless ecstasy.

I alone on the bridge, below me the helmsman
Whistling softly to the listening voicepipe,
And no sound else but the washing of the bow-wave
As the buoys go by like marching pylons.

I gaze from the glory of the bared universe
To the guarded secret of the winter world
Rapt, and the helmsman now is silent,
And I wait for the time to alter course.

To port lift the magic scenario mountains
White above the shoulders of Holy Island,
And nearer, clear as a square-lined coverlet,
All the fields and hedges on the slopes of Arran.

But further and smaller, away to starboard,
The plaited hills of Ayrshire gleam,
And I in thought am over them all
Away to my darling and my little son.

Beyond the moonlit hills that morning
My darling lay, and my little son;
But she in her cold bed lone and waking,
And he in the frozen ground asleep.

Michael Thwaites

— Drifting at Sea —

Look! my beloved, the sea-waves are rocking,
softly the eddies hurry past the boat;
here are no moments, we are not caught
in the dance of hours, and are excused
the sounding of the chimes.

For there to be time there must be sense
and consequence; the perception that rotates
in the changing of the symbol;
the opening and closing of the flower,
the scent of honeysuckle drifting in the wind,
the swoop of predatory birds
and the interminable agonizing instant
drained of precision, when the ferret
comes slinking towards the rabbit.

Such is the time of landsmen; but here
is only the continuous indifference of the sea
and the inconsequential rocking
while the cold, tireless moon
reiterates her journey in the sky.

Darrell Wilkinson

— Convoy at Night —

Moontrack silhouettes of ships gliding on the trackless deep,
pennants of white foam stealing in their wake
as the log-line reels the miles with every breath they take;
low down in deep troughs churned by surging might
bulk of a cruiser cleaves a wave in watching convoy
sight; mother to a brood of 'grey ducklings'
in the 'Med', with a waning quarter moon beaming approval
    overhead.
Stoke-hold bars are banked and black, wisps of smoke
drift from the stack. Vapour-like it idles high
dissolving sea and sky – leaving no tell-tale lie
to mark a convoy's passing by.
Sweat and turn beneath subdued glow, down 'tween decks

among a huddled row, on table form, and on cabin floor
men lie in sleep, confiding themselves to a trysting
watch crew above must keep;
spilling its human cargo on its wooded strand
as shipwrecked mariners upon island's sand, out
beneath the stars where night breezes band, through
the questing night cheerful souls dream of land;
one by one 'lanterns' die in a dimpled dawning sky,
watch is alert for dawn attack, smoke no longer filters
from the stack, to the convoy on its urgent way –
friendly night has fled, another hostile day.

William E. Morris

— Convoy —

Like lazy ducks upon a placid pond
Only deep blue, and the sun drenching
Against shadows a hard dry light, the ships rule
Whose purpose is so firm and feminine,
Now power but heart lazy, the cool limbs
Safe on a certain journey, an end sure.

Now for a moment distance intensifies
Each personal tragedy, lends wings to wish,
New favour to frail. Certain moments
Make pictures for always, continual summer
On a separate island, over each heart
An enchanted figure, someone to adore.

John Waller

— Assault Convoy —

How quietly they push the flat sea from them,
Shadows against the night, that grow to meet us
And fade back slowly to our zig-zag rhythm –
The silent pattern dim destroyers weave.
The first light greets them friendly; pasteboard ships
Erect in lineless mists of sky and sea.
A low sun lingers on the well-known outlines
That take new beauty from this sombre war-paint;
Familiar names trail childish memories
Of peace-time ports and waving, gay departures.

Only at intervals the truth breaks on us
Like catspaws, ruffling these quiet waters.
Our future is unreal, a thing to read of
Later; a chapter in a history book.
We cannot see the beaches where the dead
Must fall before this waxing moon is full;
The tracer-vaulted sky, the gun's confusion,
Searchlights and shouted orders, sweating fumbling
As landing craft are lowered; the holocaust
Grenade and bayonet will build upon these beaches.

We are dead, numbed, atrophied, sunk in the swamps of war.
Each of those thousands is a life entire.
No skilful simile can hide their sheer humanity.
Across the narrowing seas our enemies wait,
Each man the centre of his darkening world;
Bound, as we are, by humanity's traces of sorrow
To anxious women, alone in the menacing night,
Where the rhythm of Europe is lost in their private fear
And El Dorado cannot staunch their grief.

Norman Hampson

— Leaving the Med. —

We came this way before
In different ships
Which knew no casual watch.
The hills rose crimson from the brooding coast
As at the guns we watched the light's last span
Shrink with the fatal sun
To night, and eyes the night concealed
Peering from black waters.

Historical islands
Familiar as midday bombers
Pass, known by their battle names,
Islands with the dead we once had watched
When dawn was shell-plunged
Dragged by gaunt islanders down jagged graves
Or buried in torn groves.

Now leaves are green and ruins are arranged
To soothe the tourist on the languid cruise;
Bored elegance can gaze,
Admire the luscious view, the beach,
And ask, when guides are hired in hills,
Which bones are which.

We have raised periscopes
Slanting for murder
From neat waves, seen water lap blood's blue serge
From gun decks when ships screamed,
And when night's bombs had ceased,
The sick convoy, limbs floating in loose scarves,
And bobbing aimless caps.

Soon even the love we learnt will be lost,
Blotted from memory like the ports of Egypt,
Buried in obscure images of distant poetry.
This was our way.
We know faith's private history
Alone defines a way.

Michael Croft
1945

— Beach Burial —

Softly and humbly to the Gulf of Arabs
The convoys of dead sailors come;
At night they sway and wander in the waters far under,
But morning rolls them in the foam.

Between the sob and clubbing of the gunfire
Someone, it seems, has time for this,
To pluck them from the shallows and bury them in burrows
And tread the sand upon their nakedness;

And each cross, the driven stake of tidewood,
Bears the last signature of men,
Written with such perplexity, with such bewildered pity,
The words choke as they begin –

"Unknown seaman" – the ghostly pencil
Wavers and fades, the purple drips,
The breath of the wet season has washed their inscriptions
As blue as drowned men's lips,

Dead seamen, gone in search of the same landfall,
Whether as enemies they fought,
Or fought with us, or neither; the sand joins them together,
Enlisted on the other front.

Kenneth Slessor
El Alamein Beach

— 7 —
War in North West Europe: From Normandy to Berlin

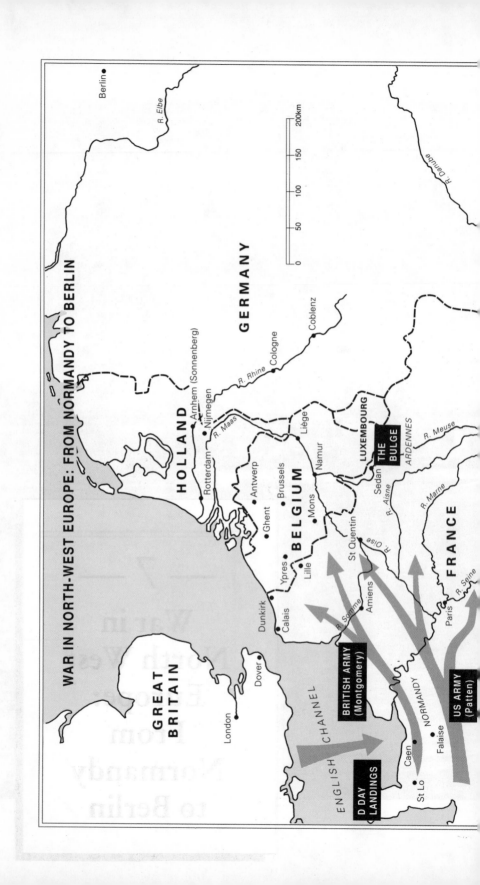

WAR IN NORTH-WEST EUROPE: FROM NORMANDY TO BERLIN

The Allies landed in Normandy in June 1944, and British tanks and infantry fought their way through the 'bocage' country of Normandy, as described by Peter Young. In 'Poor Dead Panzer' Melville Hardiment, a sergeant who led his depleted unit after the officers were killed on the Normandy beaches, shows compassion for the German who had been attacking him. At times, paratroopers filled the sky with their parachutes, but suffered heavy casualties at Arnhem where the beech trees grow, commemorated in P. A. Hyatt's 'The Weeping Beeches of Sonnenberg'. The Rhine was crossed in March and Germany surrendered in May 1945. John Buxton Hilton's 'Rest on Your Arms Reversed' mourns one more dead comrade.

— 'Love Letters of the Dead' —

A Commando Intelligence Briefing

'Go through the pockets of the enemy wounded,
Go through the pockets of the enemy dead –
There's a lot of good stuff to be found there –
That's of course if you've time,' I said.
'Love letters are specially useful,
It's amazing what couples let slip –
Effects of our bombs for example,
The size and type of a ship.
These'll all give us bits of our jigsaw.
Any questions?' I asked as per rule-book;
A close-cropped sergeant from Glasgow,
With an obstinate jut to his jaw,
Got up, and at me he pointed;
Then very slowly he said:
'Do you think it right, well I don't,
For any bloody stranger to snitch
What's special and sacred and secret,
Love letters of the dead?'

Douglas Street
Commando H.Q., December 1941

— Recce in Bocage Country[1] —

Pinned down in the sunken lane we waited
pressed into the hedgerow's shadows
and carefully encoded our location
reporting back to base our sit rep
hull-down in dead ground
in range enemy S P[2] mortar and machinegun fire
with their O P[3] two kilometres distant in church with spire.

For the landscape of war is different
admitting no valleys but re-entrants
no hollows but dead ground
churches neither gothic nor romanesque only with spire or tower;
but not lying there or sitting on our arses
we kept our head down in radio silence
dozing in the drone of bees and flies and scent of grasses.

Until we heard the beat of feet
and the soft lilt of breathy whistling
and saw the laddie with his shepherd's thumbstick
lead his dust-caked platoon snaking up the side of the lane
and halt only long enough for us to explain,
'From here you're out in the open',
and mark his map with the O P in the church with spire
and he never spoke, just nodded,
and walked on out into the searing sun
and the busy stitching of steel needles from the machinegun
with his platoon plodding behind at an easy walk
across the line of the mortar's crunching stalk.

The whistling stopped
branches broke, the lane gave a groan
and the hedgerows returned to their buzzing drone
until there came the jagged detonation of grenades
and a bren gun spoke.
Uncertain, we waited,
as boots rang out coming down the hill.

Seven came back
and threw themselves down in the shade.
'What're ye waitin' for?' one demanded.
'We've cleaned 'em out.'

So we climbed in and drove up the lane
past the laddie with his thumbstick lying under a cloud of flies
and the rest of the platoon sprawled untidily
where they'd been dropped.
'Guts,' I said. 'He must have known.'
And the reply came, flatly, 'Guts, either theirs or our own.'
For the language of war is different
and admits to no words for bravery
courage or victory
in friend or rival –
only survival.

Peter Young
1944

The rolling and wooded countryside of lower Normandy, with endless hidden lanes and
concealed tracks
Strong Point
Observation Post

— Parachute Jump —

One recalls not the moment, but the decision –
The push from a comfort of known limitations
Into the hazardous openness of a whole world.
Whipcord cold wind bangs you across fierce air,
To fall helpless, midst a blur of intensity
Till that sudden final umbilical snap.

After that it is easy, to drift, drift, drift,
Revel in the clean joy of a cloudy embrace,
Look down upon tarmac Lilliputian scramblings,
And walk sunlight through a silken limb creation
Made by many women working in dark hangars.
Cruelly those superiorities must then dissolve,
In time to brace, meet that first hard earth-shock.

Colin McIntyre

— Poor Dead Panzer —

Poor dead Panzer!
It must have cost you some
to crawl through this wheat
setting it alight,
into this ditch
where swollen flies
buzz round the stiff upturned legs
of a Uccello cart-horse:[1]
And you must have hated the stench
of which you now stink too.

Dragging your torn shoulder
through the corn, an oily smudge
on your tunic sizzling, and clutching
to your chest this evil-looking
Schmeisser machine pistol I covet,
and which sure you must have treasured
to spin round it a frothy cocoon
of brain tissues and dried blood
oozing from that hole in your forehead?

Poor old Panzer!
You sought to protect it so,
did you not? And you felt less vulnerable
with it in your hand.
Now here I am – half jew
and victorious invader –
dispossessing you.

And as I take the butt
into my plough-hands
seeking the point of balance,
I catch a whiff of Bavarian
harvest fields and temporarily
drop it back beside you.

Melville Hardiment
Epron Cross Roads,
D Day Plus 20

[1] Uccello, the Italian artist, depicted striking horses in battle-scenes

— Landscape With Tanks —

The tanks speed through the still, grey afternoon.
In drab villages straddling the road
shabby people cluster bewilderedly,
wave listlessly at the unmindful convoy.
If they raise a thin cheer, it goes unheard by the soldiers,
armour-cocooned, insulated by engine-roar, track-clatter
and their own thoughts from this winter landscape
and its sombre figures.
'Never knew about them before, did you, Corp?'
Trooper Boyce shouted to Corporal Stone,
standing beside him in an open turret.
'Knew about what?'
'Where we're going, I mean. These Ardennes,'
Boyce said and, remembering other battles,
ran the tip of his tongue over dry lips.

Jim Hovell
HQ 33 Armoured Brigade, Belgium, 1944

— Rest On Your Arms Reversed[1] —

The peace for which your comrades lived, you found:
Found all alone while they were seeking wild,
Tearing up hell for peace; true fortune's child,
You stumbled on your prize of secret ground.
Let them advance – you found your silent goal,
Untroubled by your name, your rank, your birth,
Uncalled on countless rolls; for you the Earth;
Uncried the broken prison of your soul.
Now let them cry you got their peace for them,
Let them take post to trumpet what you won;
Let them retire to live your gain undone –
You shall not tire of what dull days condemn.
When war-dreams fade, and fireside colonels fret,
Yours not to weep when humdrum men forget.

John Buxton Hilton
Berlin, Winter 1945

A drill movement used at funerals with the rifle swung upside down

— The Question —

Perhaps I killed a man to-day,
   I cannot tell: I do not know,
But bare three hundred yards away,
   Where weeping willows grow,
Fell sudden silence on the heels
   Of my last shot, whose echoes rang
Along the Rhine. A silence steals
   Across the river, save the bang
Of distant, screaming shell;
   The tapping of the Spandau
Comes no more; brief quiet fell
   Where weeping willows grow.

Perhaps I killed a man to-day,
   The secret's hid, forever laid
Among those willows o'er the way;
   Here, beneath the quiet shade
Of a heeled, abandoned tank,
   I fired across the river,
   Made water ripples shiver,
     And perhaps I killed a man
Upon that distant bank.

Who am I to play at fate,
To aim, and fire, and arbitrate
'Tween life and death; not knowing hate,
   To send with sad, departing whine
   Irrevocable death across the Rhine.
The willows answer not. The scent
Of clover lingered while I went
   Between the fields where ruins stand;
   Dead horses lie along the land,
   Who died, and did not understand
Why this should be; no more may I
Explain why any man should die.
And still I fired; and wonder why.

Alexander McKee
Nijmegen, April 1945

— Rhine Jump, 1944 —

They dropped us on the guns, left us in a flaring
lurch of slipstream kicking like sprayed flies, –
till canopies shook sudden heads, inhaled, held
   a breath, –
alive again we slanted down,
too many, into their doomed sights.

One scrambled moment it was red, green,
dragging to the door of the Douglas[1] then
falling through a monstrous aviary roof
on Guy Fawkes Night (only this was day)
into shrill scarifying glory . . .

then Germany, the Fatherland, a zooming field –
banged down on it, stood up among the chaos, with
fingers flopped like rubber gloves trying
to slap one's box, slough the afterbirth of chute,
make somehow that snatch of wood.

There were chutes already in those trees, caught:
battalion boys who'd dropped too late or drifted . . .
harness-ravelled, cocooned there –
like silkworms, moveless, wet . . .
so easy, against all that white.

But not so many resistive earthworms –
the early birds had seen to that.
Soon, it was rendezvous: a stodgy farm.
The war was folding: fight-thin.
Prisoners happened; columned, toneless.

Next day it was hearing tales again,
having a kip in a pigsty, scouting the dropping-zone
to get silk (knickers for sweethearts, wives);
maybe a green envelope, speculation
about leave, Japan.

Oh and a gun-pit by the way, an 88:
bodiless, nothing special, –
only the pro's interest in other's kit:
grey slacks for the use of, old, ersatz;
with a brown inside stripe: non-ersatz.

Geoffrey Holloway

[1] An American transport-plane

— The Weeping Beeches of Sonnenberg[1] —

Ankle deep in old dead leafs
I strode among the stately beech trees
of this old battlefield,
Anguish in my heart.
I wept for long dead comrades,
I wept for the peace and silence
In these dark woods where trees,
like my soul, are scarred and pitted with old wounds.

The melancholy anguish I have carried these many years
Those boys I killed (shall I ever be forgiven?)
I see those boys every waking day,
the grey green uniforms,
their white marble, dead faces.
People say 'why do you grieve, they would have killed first'
Would that I had been killed first,
than bequeathed with a life of guilt.

Those questions I put to the trees,
they answer, 'Why do you grieve so?
Did you not leave us shattered, torn and broken,
swathes of destruction left through us?
But look at us now, Look well my friend
for we are regrown and reborn,
Look closer, see we still carry scars.'

Mute and silent I ponder this.
Closer I looked and noticed the trees too were weeping,
but not with my anguished weeping.
They wept for joy.
Small nodules each with a tear duct I noticed everywhere,
Each nodule a piece of shrapnel ejected and rejected.
As they rejected they wept for joy, reaching up to the sky
and joyfully rejecting the iron from the soul.
And so the trees have repaired, regrown,
Deep and lovely are the groves of weeping beeches of Sonnenberg.

P. A. Hyatt
4th Ind Para Brigade, 1st Airborne Division,
Arnhem/Oosterbeek 1944

[1] War cemetery near Arnhem. Each year veterans of Arnhem return for a pilgrimage and pick up the fallen leaves of the beeches of Sonnenberg.

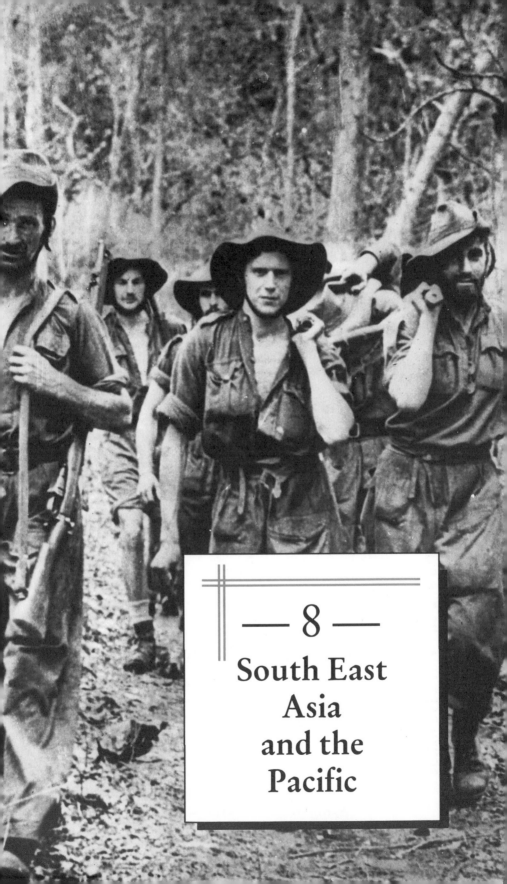

South East Asia and the Pacific

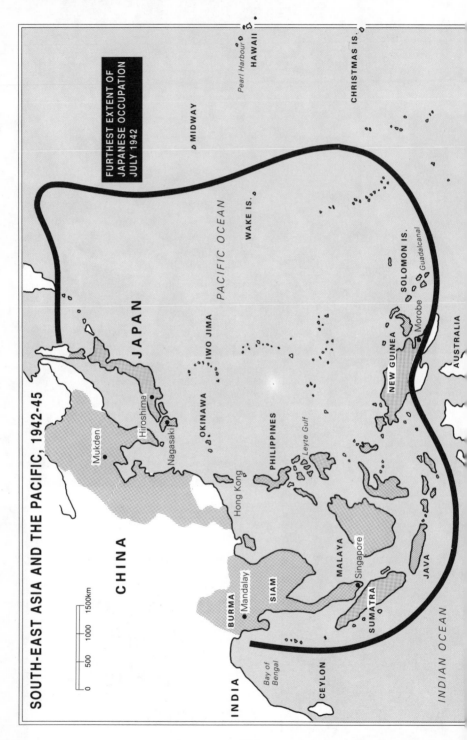

SOUTH-EAST ASIA AND THE PACIFIC, 1942-45

FURTHEST EXTENT OF
JAPANESE OCCUPATION
JULY 1942

CHINA

JAPAN

INDIA

Bay of
Bengal

CEYLON

BURMA

SIAM

Mandalay

Mukden

Hiroshima

Nagasaki

Hong Kong

MALAYA

Singapore

SUMATRA

JAVA

MIDWAY

PACIFIC OCEAN

WAKE IS.

IWO JIMA

OKINAWA

PHILIPPINES

Leyte Gulf

NEW GUINEA

Morobe

SOLOMON IS.

Guadalcanal

AUSTRALIA

INDIAN OCEAN

Pearl Harbour

HAWAII

CHRISTMAS IS.

0 500 1000 1500km

This theatre of war comprised both the South East mainland, including India, Burma and Malaya, and the Pacific, so there are poems about the steamy jungle by Alun Lewis and George Richardson, and about the insect-ridden island of Morobe by the Australian Eric Oxley. George Shepperson's 'Askari Song' offers a different perspective from Africa. Towards the end of the war, the Japanese, who had taken Singapore so easily, were gradually forced back, leaving many dead, and inspiring such poems as Bernard Gutteridge's 'The Enemy Dead' and Charles McCausland's 'Dead Japanese'. But these are sad poems with no hatred or celebration; their poets were not flag-waving warriors.

— The Fortress of the East[1] —

A MIGHTY ISLAND FORTRESS
THE GUARDIAN OF THE EAST
IMPREGNABLE AS GIBRALTAR A
THOUSAND PLANES AT LEAST
IT SIMPLY CAN'T BE TAKEN
IT'LL STAND A SIEGE FOR YEARS
WE'LL HOLD THE PLACE FOREVER
IT WILL BRING THE JAPS TO TEARS
OUR MEN ARE THERE IN THOUSANDS
DEFENCES ARE UNIQUE
THE JAPS DID NOT BELIEVE IT
AND TOOK IT IN A WEEK.

Anonymous

[1] Singapore

— The Jungle (extract) —

In mole-blue indolence the sun
Plays idly on the stagnant pool
In whose grey bed black swollen leaf
Holds Autumn rotting like an unfrocked priest.
The crocodile slides from the ochre sand
And drives the great translucent fish
Under the boughs across the running gravel.
Windfalls of brittle mast crunch as we come
To quench more than our thirst – our selves –
Beneath this bamboo bridge, this mantled pool
Where sleep exudes a sinister content
As though all strength of mind and limb must pass
And all fidelities and doubts dissolve,
The weighted world a bubble in each head,
The warm pacts of the flesh betrayed
By the nonchalance of a laugh,
The green indifference of this sleep.

II

Wandering and fortuitous the paths
We followed to this rendezvous today
Out of the mines and offices and dives,
The sidestreets of anxiety and want,
Huge cities known and distant as the stars,
Wheeling beyond our destiny and hope.
We did not notice how the accent changed
As shadows ride from precipice to plain
Closing the parks and cordoning the roads,
Clouding the humming cultures of the West –
The weekly bribe we paid the man in black,
The day shift sinking from the sun,
The blinding arc of rivets blown through steel,
The patient queues, headlines and slogans flung
Across a frightened continent, the town
Sullen and out of work, the little home
Semi-detached, suburban, transient
As fever or the anger of the old,
The best ones on some specious pretext gone.

But we who dream beside this jungle pool
Prefer the instinctive rightness of the poised

Pied kingfisher deep darting for a fish
To all the banal rectitude of states,
The dew-bright diamonds on a viper's back
To the slow poison of a meaning lost
And the vituperations of the just.

Alun Lewis

[DECEMBER 22ND, 1943]
*I went on a three-hundred-mile journey last week to look at
the jungle. It was a unique experience. You enter a separate
world, remote, unperturbed, indifferent, serene; and it makes
your own troubles and fears fall away and remain outside in
the world of roads and spaces . . .*
[JANUARY 5TH, 1944]
*I've been in the bush all day. There's a river of long idle pools
and huge white boulders a mile or so in the forest. I've bathed
in it every day so far. But as we broke on to it this morning on
a compass march, lo! sleeping on a spit of red sand was a great
crocodile. He slid into the pool like a quiet thought, hardly
stirring the water. It's such a bewildering country, parts of it
are as peaceful and quiet as Penbryn – yet it contains all the
coldness and pride of nature, elephants and bison, tigers,
reptiles and insects. I love it.*

from Letters from India *by Alun Lewis*

Alun Lewis died on the Arakan front on March 5th, 1944.

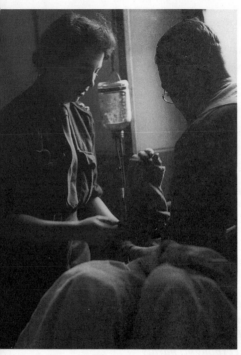

— Bengal Summer —

Egrets haunt the memory,
    Large snow-white birds with green stick legs
Whose delicate feathered crests
    Rise and fall like Geishas' fans.
Cormorants too abound,
    Black as night, advertising their presence
With a powerful odour of fish
    And a carpet of ivory bones.

The frangipani trees
    Swoon in the heat, shedding waxen petals,
Fragrant as the silken saris
    The high-caste women wear.
Sharp against the sky
    A gibbet tree hangs with strange blossom,
The ragged frames of fruit-bats
    Awaiting the coming of night.

Angela Bolton
May 194

Angela Bolton trained as a nurse and was posted to South East Asia, where she
nursed in tented hospitals similar to this one

— Malayan Malady —

Oh! how I hate this tropic land,
Its burning sun, its baking sand,
Its heavy, humid, sticky heat,
With odorous decay replete.
I hate the feathery coconut trees
Languidly drowsing in the breeze,
The frangipani's cloying smell
And all the other smells as well.

The tropic moonlight leaves me cold,
And all the myriad stars untold;
The rubber trees – unlovely whores

With obscene scars and running sores –
The black sumatra's sudden rain;
The tom-tom's maddening refrain;
In none of these, for me at least,
Appears the glamour of the East.

I hate the morning's blinding light,
I hate the suffocating night,
I hate the listless afternoons,
I hate the dark that comes too soon.
The amorous cheechak's[1] plaintive trill,
The cricket's serenading shrill,
The whining mossies round my net
Have failed to fascinate me yet.

I hate the khaki tunic drab,
The stupid spurs, the scarlet tab,
The portly blokes in naval rig
Who execute a stately jig,
The army subs. with weak moustache,
The RAF so short of cash,
The colonels' and the captains' wives,
The smug intrigue, the double lives.

The ceaseless quest for quick romance,
The shuffling mob at a Raffles' dance,
The curry tiffins, evening pahits,[2]
The blaring bands and shaded lights,
The futile trek from flick to hop,
The floorshows at the Cathay Top,
The shrivelled dames, the men obese,
From all of these I crave release . . .

Yes! how I hate this sunny clime,
The wanton waste of precious time,
The unmarked flight of heedless days,
Faces that vanish in a haze
Of half-forgotten memories dim,
The apathetic boredom grim,
In all its aspects, fair and bland,
By God! I hate this goddam land.

George S. Richardson

[1] Lizard
[2] Drinks

— Morobe[1] —

The sandflies they attack you
And the mossies they ack-ack you,
And sing a little ditty in your ear.
They chuckle with elation
And attack you in formation,
Till you curse and swear and wipe away your tear.

With the comin' of the mornin',
Just another day is dawnin',
The same routine is on again once more,
The 'dengues'[2] buzz around you
And scream 'Ha-Ha' we've found you,
Then dive bomb you from twenty feet or more.

Then you think of dough you've wasted,
And beer that you have tasted,
With steak and eggs and schooners by the score.
When you think of fun you're missin'
Or some sheila you'd be kissin',
Boy, you wish they up and end this bloody war.

Eric A. Oxley
Morobe, New Guinea, 1943

[1] An island off New Guinea
[2] Mosquitoes that carry dengue fever

— Indian Soldiers Singing —

I

On a narrow jungle path
in single file they march.
Not a word disturbs
the people of sun.
The silence of noonday doldrums seems death to me
where snake or the enemy lurks, where thirst tugs
and sweat drips smarting in the eyes without a pause.
I look not for a sign beyond the heat of day

but a thin strain quivers and rises in the sky
and fills all heaven in a mocking melody;
   sound falls loud and profound
   on tangled trees and steaming ground –
Lord Krishna,[1] your soldiers in the jungle sing!

A soldier's voice climbs like a lark to sing,
   stays as a hawk hovering,
filling the whole world a moment with song,
   then falling, his earthly measure filled,
     his voice is still;
but the round sound of the rhythmic marching band
rolls through the mid-day miles –
Lord Krishna, singing
   all Brahmanda's praise.[2]

II

O spirit of love and longing for my day
these sudden voices in the jungle raise
all my hope in to a height of joy
and utter understanding of their song;
these singing soldiers on this jungle path
are one in the world with me now.

Yet all endeavour has an end, and song
like momentary vision dies; it leaves me now
all in a soundless muse and wondering.

III

   Lord Krishna, soldiers die
     and singing has to cease!
   Lord Krishna, shall we sing again?
     O dying song is sorrowful!
     O stay the singing in our hearts!

You came, Lord Krishna, from the silent hills
   and followed us among the jungle trees;
     and shall you be, Lord Krishna,
      in the stone streets of London
      and on the lonely seas?

Peter Russell
Lower Burma, July 1945

[1] Great Hindu God
[2] Praise of the Supreme Being

— Askari Song: Airdrop[1] —

Amai, [2]
Amai,
The great Brown Bird on high:
Amai,
Amai,
Amai watu.[3]

Cruel the Zungus[4] and weird their ways –
But for their Brown Bird we have only praise,
Dropping white flowers of food from high,
A trail of stars along an empty sky.

We have known hunger, starvation in peace, till
Now, in war, near death, our bellies fill
Amai, let the Bird be very close at hand
When we are back in our Nyasaland.

Amai,
Amai,
The great Brown Bird on high:
Amai,
Amai,
Amai watu.

George Shepperson

[1] Nyasaland African soldiers sang about everything – even about Dakotas supplying the forces in Burma with food
[2] Mother (Nyanja language)
[3] Our mother
[4] White men

— The Enemy Dead —

The dead are always searched.
It's not a man, the blood-soaked
Mess of rice and flesh and bones
Whose pockets you flip open;
And these belongings are only
The counterpart to scattered ball
Or the abandoned rifle.

Yet later the man lives.
His postcard of a light blue
Donkey and sandy minarets
Reveals a man at last.
'Object – the panther mountains!
Two – a tired soldier of Kiku![1]
Three – my sister the bamboo sigh!

Then again the man dies.
And only what he has seen
And felt, loved and feared
Stays as a hill, a soldier, a girl:
Are printed in the skeleton
Whose white bones divide and float away
Like nervous birds in the sky.

Bernard Gutteridge

[1] Of the Japanese Emperor. *Kiku* is the Japanese word for the chrysanthemum, the emblem of the royal family

— Dead Japanese —

Why does your pointing finger accuse,
your black arm, swollen (skin stretched tight
as a surgeon's glove) point, accuse?
Was your cause just
that you accuse me, your enemy?
You the aggressor, I the defender?

Why do you stink so, fouling the air, the grass,
the stagnant pool in the creek?
No other animal stinks so in putrefaction.
Why do you vent your protest against life itself?
Is it seemly for the dead to fight?

Have you not known the sun,
the sweet softness of a woman's breasts,
rest after work?

Then let your arm drop to your side, as in deep sleep;
hasten your decay, sink into the earth,
unloosing your last hold on personality
to know, unknowing, every man's rebirth
in other life; so, when the winds pass, you may be
part of the sweetness of the rippling kunai grass.

Charles McCausland
New Guinea, 1943

— 9 —

Behind the Wire

Prisoners of War had time to write, as Uys Krige's 'Midwinter'
shows, but they sometimes lacked the means, and exercise books
were often lost in inspections and treks from camp to camp,
especially in the later stages of the war in Europe when the Germans
moved prisoners around repeatedly. Roger Rothwell in Japanese
hands actually scrounged officers' loo paper to write on, which he
bound into a book and hid under the floorboards. To be caught
risked death. These are poems of confinement and hunger and often
of cruel death. John Durnford saw his comrades die in the
Chungkai Camp, and Frederick Rackstraw somehow managed to
write 'Last Post' while working on the Burma Railway. In Germany
Dr Phillip Whitfield treated prisoners as they were liberated from
Belsen. His poem is that of the eye-witness.

— Midwinter —

Gone are the mountains, gone Il Gran Sasso,[1] every peak, every
    cliff and outcrop, gaunt and black, craggy hard
swallowed by the mist;
and gone the fresh little mole mounds, no sooner heaped up than
    beaded with frost, here in the prison yard
no bigger than my fist.

Gone too the country-roads like rods of ebony that cut these
    fields of snow into strict squares of black and white,
rigid rectangles;
and gone the tiny tracks of snails that looped themselves round a
    clean cobblestone shining as beautiful and bright
as jingling bangles,
spooring the gutter's edge, crisscrossing the mess-kitchen steps,
    sparkling even in this crude half light
with the sheen of spangles.
And from the eaves the long, sharp-pointed icicle – winter's
    dagger with hilt and shaft silver-chased – stabbing the sight
no longer dangles.

We have come to the dead-end of all our days, all our nights:
    these four blank walls a drab red brown by day, pitch black by
    night. There is no turning
backward or forward from this.
This is our life, our death-in-life: this gloom, this ghostly pallor

above each cot at noon, this cold at day's meridian, as cold as
ice but burning, burning
even as war's embrace, the blazing battle's bitter kiss.

Through the chinks, the cracks in the wide wooden door, the
   shattered window, the mist seeps. Its wisps cluster, drift and veer
above each wooden bed.
The floor is of cement. There is no stove or fire. In two long
   rows we lie freezing under our blankets. In this grey
   whiteness lingering around us, drooping, drear,
from which all speech, all sound has fled,
no one speaks. All the old battles, desert scraps, dogfights,
   crashes on the desert's deck, swimming around in the cold,
   dark Med before the slow red dawn, all the heroism and
   gallantry, all the cowardice and the horror and the fear,
nothing, nothing has been left unsaid.

We have come to the end of all our small talk, our tether, our
   high hopes, ambitions. We have exhausted even the
   bickerings, the stupid quarrels, the sneer, the snarl. We have
   foregone all that we loved, cherished, held most dear
and all our books are read.

Uys Krige
Prisoner of War Camp No. 78, Italy

[1] The highest part of the Apennines, north of Aguila

Later Uys Krige escaped from this camp.

— Oflag Night Piece, Colditz —

('The poor man's wealth, the prisoner's release' – Sir Philip Sidney)

There, where the swifts flicker along the wall
And the last light catches, there in the high schloss[1]
(How the town grows dark) all's made impregnable.
They bless each window with a double cross
Of iron; weave close banks of wire and train
Machine guns down on them; and look – at the first star
Floodlight the startled darkness back again . . .
All for three hundred prisoners of war.
Yet now past them and the watch they keep,
Unheard, invisible, in ones and pairs.
In groups, in companies – alarms are dumb,
A sentry loiters, a blind searchlight stares –
Unchallenged as their memories of home
The vanishing prisoners escape to sleep.

Michael Riviere

[1] Castle (German) – Colditz was a castle on a hill

All the officers in the picture, except myself, were taken prisoner in France in 1940. Douglas Moir, of the Royal Tank Regiment, despite five years as a prisoner of war, remained in the Army and became a Colonel. James Mellor and David Walker, 51st Highland Division, were taken prisoner at St. Valery on the French coast, providing the diversion from Dunkirk. Captain David Walker of the Black Watch had been A.D.C. to the Governor General of Canada just before the War. Of those listed below, 'still at large', Patrick Campbell Preston (mis-recorded by the Germans), also of the Black Watch, later commanded his regiment; I doubt if the David Hamilton mentioned was Ian Baillie-Hamilton who, with Captain Frank Weldon, engineered the Eichstatt tunnel through which about 60 of us escaped and who later became a Brigadier.

No-one from that tunnel got right away. The Germans were so alarmed at 60 British officers escaping together that they mobilised their Home Guard, throughout Bavaria and we were all picked up within a week. I was caught four nights later trying to cross the Danube to joint the Yugoslav partisans. We spent the rest of the war in Colditz.

Note by Michael Riviere on the German WANTED Notice

Pictures to accompany 4603a of the German Criminal Police gazette

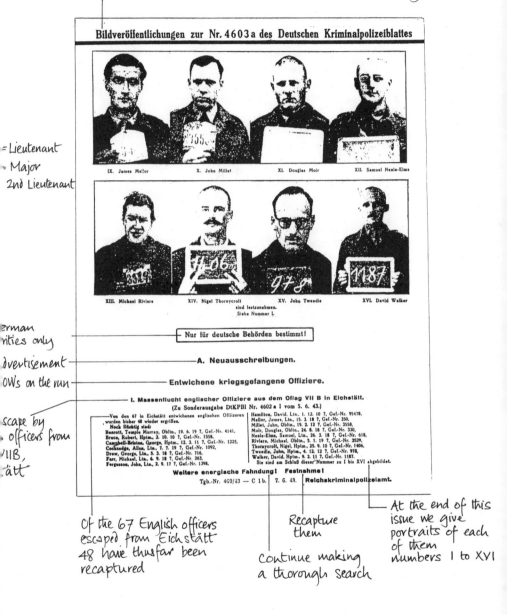

Bildveröffentlichungen zur Nr. 4603a des Deutschen Kriminalpolizeiblattes

IX. James Mellor
X. John Millet
XI. Douglas Moir
XII. Samuel Neale-Elms

XIII. Michael Riviere
XIV. Nigel Thornycroft
sind festzunehmen.
Siehe Nummer I.
XV. John Tweedie
XVI. David Walker

Nur für deutsche Behörden bestimmt!

A. Neuausschreibungen.

Entwichene kriegsgefangene Offiziere.

I. Massenflucht englischer Offiziere aus dem Oflag VII B in Eichstätt.
(Zu Sonderausgabe DtKPBl Nr. 4602a I vom 5. 6. 43.)

Von den 67 in Eichstätt entwichenen englischen Offizieren wurden bisher 48 wieder ergriffen.
Noch flüchtig sind:

Bearott, Temple Murray, Obltn., 19. 6. 19 7, Gef.-Nr. 4141,
Bruce, Robert, Hptm., 2. 10. 10 7, Gef.-Nr. 1558,
Campbell-Bristos, George, Hptm., 12. 3. 11 7, Gef.-Nr. 1225,
Cockredge, Allan, Ltn., 7. 7. 19 7, Gef.-Nr. 1092,
Drew, George, Ltn., 5. 3. 18 7, Gef.-Nr. 716,
Farr, Michael, Ltn., 6. 9. 18 7, Gef.-Nr. 263,
Fergusson, John, Ltn., 2. 9. 17 7, Gef.-Nr. 1398,

Hamilton, David, Ltn., 1. 12. 10 7, Gef.-Nr. 95478,
Mellor, James, Ltn., 15. 3. 18 7, Gef.-Nr. 350,
Millet, John, Obltn., 19. 2. 12 7, Gef.-Nr. 3558,
Moir, Douglas, Obltn., 24. 8. 18 7, Gef.-Nr. 330,
Neale-Elms, Samuel, Ltn., 26. 3. 18 7, Gef.-Nr. 618,
Riviere, Michael, Oblt., 5. 1. 19 7, Gef.-Nr. 3529,
Thornycroft, Nigel, Hptm., 25. 9. 10 7, Gef.-Nr. 1406,
Tweedie, John, Hptm., 4. 12. 12 7, Gef.-Nr. 978,
Walker, David, Hptm., 9. 2. 11 7, Gef.-Nr. 1187.
Sie sind am Schluß dieser Nummer zu I bis XVI abgebildet.

Weitere energische Fahndung! Festnahme!
Tgb.-Nr. 469/43 — C 1 b. | 7. 6. 43. | Reichskriminalpolizeiamt.

= Lieutenant
= Major
2nd Lieutenant

German [authorities] only

[ad]vertisement

[P]OWs on the run

[e]scape by [?] officers from [V]IIB, [Eichst]ätt

Of the 67 English officers escaped from Eichstätt 48 have thusfar been recaptured

Recapture them

Continue making a thorough search

At the end of this issue we give portraits of each of them numbers I to XVI

A PRAYER FOR FOOD.

Lord, I have asked You once before
To send more food into the store,
To send us something really nice –
Not just chrysanthemums and rice.
I asked for meat and lard (or ghi)
And parcels from the B.R.C.[1]
But that was several weeks ago
And nothing has been sent, You know.
It may be that you didn't hear
Or else because good food is dear
Though if you shopped at our Canteen
You'd know what prices really mean.
You know, Lord that we're on our uppers
With only rice "bas" for our suppers,
And that many through this process
Have got this avitaminosis.[2]
And some pallagra[3] too, and very
Many have got beri-beri.
While others that I have in mind
Have gone stone-deaf or nearly blind.
I tell You, Lord, there's hundreds who
Would sell their souls for Irish stew.
I'm sure you've done it for the best,
To see how we should stand the test;
But don't you think we've stuck it well
Through two years pretty average hell –
As far as food's concerned at least –
I don't count thyamine[4] or yeast,
For what we need to cure our ills
Is solid food, not drugs and pills.
A Yorkshire ham, a dozen eggs,
Would cure the aching in our legs;
And chunks of beef are better far
Than pills of Wakamoto[5] are
To drive our aches and pains away.
So please, Lord, send without delay
Some meat and bread and eggs and cheese
And if you really want to please,
A crate or so of Guinness' Stout
To fill our scrawny muscles out.

27.2.44

Roger Rothwell
Bowen Road Hospital POW Camp

[1] British Red Cross
[2] Vitamin deficiency
[3] Deficiency disease
[4] Vitamin B
[5] Vitamin pills

Written on stolen Japanese officer's toilet paper, made up into a diary, and hidden in the camp.

'Argyle Street', Prisoner of War Camp N., Hong Kong – sketch by K. Sawyer

'. . . our diet consisted of a daily ration of between 6 to 12 ounces of dry rice – according to whether or not we were under punishment for one of our many misdeeds – and a weekly issue of vegetables – mainly lettuce, chrysanthemums, leaves and stalks and sweet potato tops – all of which had to be boiled because of the risk of cholera and dysentery. There was never any sugar, fat or meat, only occasionally some tiny bony fish which were caught at the mouth of the sewage outfall and, as a result, nearly everyone suffered from beri-beri and pellagra, typical diseases of malnutrition.'

In a letter from Roger Rothwell

— Last Post —

(Written while working on the Burma Railway 1942–44)

The camp is noisy, with the shouts of men's laughter and curses,
With the whining grumble about the orders, the food and the lice!
From every attap hut[1] the steady mumble of a thousand
    discussions of the stale news.
The clop of wooden slippers, the rattle of a pail, and someone
    banging bamboo slats for bugs.
The slither of impatient feet in meal queues
And the clanging din of tin plates, mess tins and mugs.
Suddenly, from the graveyard the clear arresting bugle races
    through the uproar,
Like a summer breeze that bends the golden wheatear in the field,
So that the inattentive stalks are by their neighbours bent over
    with a shudder,
All straighten and are still!
In the camp with notes come loud and clear –
'Psst! Quiet there! Last post!'
Hot words are left unspoken, a hand half way arrested –
Hurrying feet freeze into immobility,
Then a deep and awful silence settles
Now the camp is still –
Only the clear notes of the bugle go soaring above the jungle to
    the sky . . .
Then with a loud sigh the spell is broken
There is a shuffle of feet on sand
A rustle and a bustle, a growing hustle, laughs, shouts and
    arguments,
And clanking billy cans!

                                    Frederick Rackstraw

[1] Shelter roofed with palm or bamboo leaves

— Lying Awake at Night —

When men die here I am afraid –
Death takes no ceremonial leave
With horse and foot, in a parade
Acceptable to those that grieve,
The silver, and the glossy plumes,
The solemn uniforms, slow tread
Of soldiery, the stifled drums

That make one doubt a man were dead;
Here only the owls betray the grave,
Only the yews are evidence
Of what rich marrow ever gave
Their roots strange sustenance.

When men die here I am afraid –
Too much lies buried deep, too deep
The ancient soil is over-laid
With blood, too many armies sleep
In the same ground unaware;
Too many times the hideous priests
Hallowed their sacrifices where
These thickets stand; too many feasts
Were held on these high places, since
Obliterated by the rain;
Too often has a Burman prince
Slaughtered his heroes in this plain.

When men die here I am afraid –
The night is motionless and still,
Each minute afterwards is made
More silent by the cricket's shrill
Interruption. Sleepless lie
The listeners. Wild dogs keen
In the shuttered village, the whole sky
Shakes with the pinions and obscene
Gloating of vultures, and no moon
Discloses to the frightened skies
The obscure agonies so soon
Changed into birth before our eyes. . . .

But I believe each death conceives
And bears new children, and a store
Of great fertility derives
From every grave. For into them
Only untraceable remains
Without reality or name
Are ever lowered. Who maintains
With any certainty indeed
Anything but that a kindly spade
Turns over soil for ever made
More fertile by another seed?

John Durnford
Chungkai, December 1943

— 133 —

— Day of Liberation, Bergen–Belsen, May 1945 —

We build our own prison walls
but that day the doors fell open,
it was holiday time
in the death camp.

Lift him with courtesy,
this silent survivor.
Battle-dress doctors,
we took him from the truck
and put him to bed.

The moving skeleton
had crippled hands,
his skinny palms held secrets:
when I undid the joints I found
five wheat grains huddled there.
In the faces of other people
I witness my distress.

I close my eyes:
ten thousand wasted people
still piled in the flesh-pits.
Death of one is the death of all.
It is not the dead I pity.

Phillip Whitfield

'I was somewhat unexpectedly posted to Belsen and there were
a great many problems not only inside but outside the camp.
Once the camp was liberated of course anyone who could
stagger staggered out. That is the natural inclination, is it not?
And you probably, if you were in that state, you collapsed after
a few yards or a mile – I mean a whole lot of them had typhus
and my job was to collect them . . . The war is an experience
and I've never been the same person since because of it.'

Phillip Whitfield

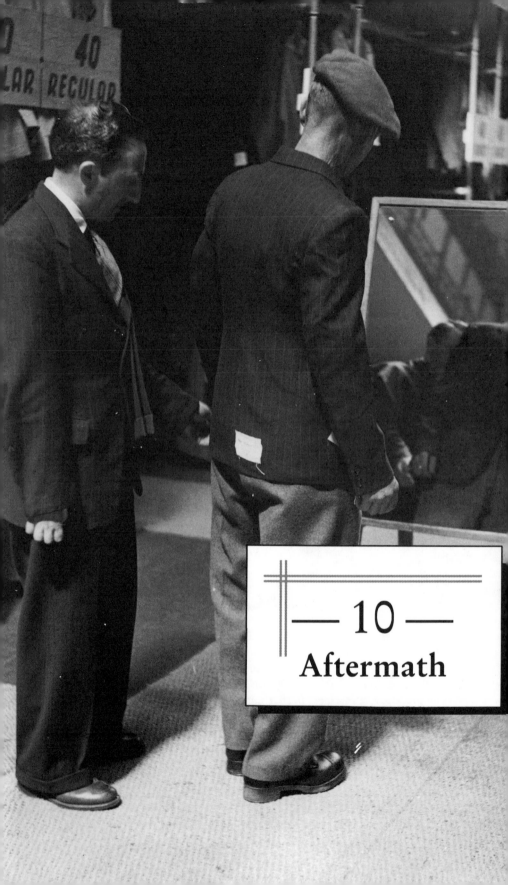

— 10 —
Aftermath

As the war ends Robin Ivy follows the 8th Army from war to peace in Austria. Joy Corfield learns of civilian life; F. A. Horn has mixed feelings about leaving the army, and Norman Maxwell Dunn finds a lack of welcome back home in Australia. John Warry and Ian Fletcher reflect on those left behind, and Frank Thompson's *'Polliciti Meliora'* prophesies his own death, shot in Bulgaria. The poems end with the end of War as the world then knew it, with the dropping of the Atomic Bomb on Japan, an event questioned in Edward Lowbury's 'August 10th, 1945 – The Day After'. He asks 'Who ... has power to pass such sentence?' Victor West's 'The Victors' and Michael Armitage's 'The Meadow' also ask questions about war and its consequences.

— Italy to Austria —

We knew that peace had come
When driving down the steady tree lined road –
No traffic jams of tanks and guns
Or silent men on foot.
No long delays
When urgent jeeps would slip between:
No bridges blown,
No signs to say that dust brings shells
Or maddening roughly-worn diversions –
We knew that peace had come
Because the convoys one by one
Clocked by at leisured speed,
And in the fields
The trucks were parked in squares,
Patiently awaiting their return
After the dust and thunder of the years.

Robin Ivy

— The Victors —

They had talked of nothing else
but the fishing to be had.
At the Turn-Off for Bayreuth,
our Jeep stopped and we stood down
on rubbery legs, grateful for the lift.
We gave them the fish that bomb-happy
Major had taken out the Naab with dynamite.

Belting seven bells out the road to Prague,
Red Ball expresses hurtled towards us,
beflouring all with dust.
                              The day advanced our drought.
Max indicated where a neat farmhouse lay back
off the road, *'Hier mann trinkt wasser, bitte?'*[1]
Suspicious, the old farmer motioned us to wait
in large room while his frau brought us milk.
This, the scene of many family feasts and jollity –
now austere as workhouse ... or a shrine, perhaps.
As we drank, smiling faces of the young watched,
each from simple black frame: *'Geffalen für der Führer'*[2]
all around, all gone those past years of madness.
No children scampered before us, as we left
sadly musing, disconcerted victors, tails between legs.

Victor West
Franconian Jura, 25 April 1945

[1] 'Can we have some water, please?' (German)
[2] 'Died for the Fuhrer.' (German)

*The Red Ball Express was a convoy of non-stop lorries bringing
petrol, ammunition and rations to Patton's 3rd Army, halted
on its drive to Prague. This we saw on the military road. It
gave me the chance to swap my Luger for 'K' rations (a
pre-packed carton of food for an American front line soldier,
containing instant coffee, a candy bar and two cigarettes to last
the day) to march on. You can't eat a pistol.*

Victor West

— Let's Go Back —

(This was written in a moment of cynicism shortly after arriving home)

Do you think, if we asked nicely, for a passage back
　To the German prison camps we know so well,
That the Gov'ment would allow it – or would they still insist
　We endure our homeland's 'welcome' from that Hell.

For years in those surroundings, we dreamed of our return,
　And we built our simple castles in the air:
We'd buy a home and furnish, or we'd rent a little flat,
　And we'd find goodwill a-plenty everywhere.

We've heard so many speeches, and read so many plans,
　We're sure our sons are going to be alright:
But it's so draughty reading papers in the street,
　Right now we're more concerned with our own plight.

The Germans gave us shelter, crowded though it was,
　While Australia gives us nothing – 'cept some cheers.
She's very glad to see us, and hopes we'll hang around,
　'We may need you boys again in future years!'

We're coming in our thousands, from the fronts and camps,
　From Jap and German strongholds far away:
And we find you've failed us badly – as you have failed before,
　Seems like you didn't expect us back to stay!

So when you give your welcomes, and when you play your
　　bands,
　Forgive us if we smile a little, please,
You can call us little heroes, and tell us what you've done,
　But we did have huts to live in – overseas.

Norman Maxwell Dunn
Australia, 19 September 1945

— Release Group Blues —

In the drab shape of khaki, four dead years
I've spent in this damned place, four bloody years
Of slime and heartbreak, guards and graft and grime,
Of flagrant exploitation all the time,
Of Jacks-in-office, idiots in charge,
Headaches, and tortured limbs, and fools at large,
Administration crazy, cretin's rule,
The nadir of existence – Mars' poor tool.

Dreaming of freedom, scant escape I found
Scourging with pleasures fragments of the day
That discipline discarded; now the ground
Is covered, and escape is sure. The way
To freedom opens. I am glad – I know;
Yet here's the rub – I hate like hell to go!

F. A. Horn
13 February 1946

— Friends Gone —

Philip's slim half-forgotten hand-writing
And Donald courting death like a girl
And Tony when drunk finding God exciting
And Peter whose courtship was too successful

Falling down in a locket of fire;
And Kenneth with his sinister metaphysic;
Jack Gregory loving his gun and his beer
With one or two others out of the wreck
Fashioning some vivid life of their own.

Now what I remember, what runs quick
Round the heart is this much alone:
Some found that death was too lovely, or
Some were bent on trying to believe it so,
Some merely stayed away, uncalled for:
Their time was shortest, having nowhere to go.

Ian Fletcher

— Budget for Romance —

I fell in love with a sergeant
So took a course in domestic virtues
In Bad Oeynhausen.[1]
The girls in the class
Were drawn from different units
But we shared romantic dreams
Of being super wives and mothers.
They taught us to cook, to clean and mend,
They lectured us on health, on sex and children:
They pointed out the problems
Of finding a home and how to equip it
Worst of all was 'The Budget'.
From our future husband's income
We deducted rent, food and heating,
With other essentials.
Only one girl could make it balance.
Her future husband was an electrician
And would earn £5 a week.
We were envious of her good luck.
We thought her life free from care.

Joy Corfield

[1] A town in North Germany

— War Graves —

White galaxies of war graves chalk the way
From Flanders southwards to the Libyan coast.
Quiet neighbours dwell in the disputed clay
And none of them now cares who won or lost.
Young men who killed each other in the sky
Share narrow churchyards under English yews.
No rhetoric can reach them where they lie,
No commentaries appended to the news.
Yet why should I declare them innocent
And lay the blame upon authority
With eulogies of general extent
Slyly contrived to cover you and me?
We are all guilty. Only, don't forget
That they have paid and we have not – not yet.

John Warry

— August 10th, 1945 – The Day After[1] —

Who will be next to break this terrible silence,
While the doom of war still shivers over these
Unwilling either to die or to be defeated, –
In the agony of death still torn, contorted,
Torn between saving face and body, both
Mutilated almost beyond recognition?
The face fights on long after
The body's overwhelmed and hacked to pieces.
Every scar of it's their fault; yet I am dumb;
In the blind eyes of pity the good and the evil
Are equals when they're gasping in the sand,
Helpless. The reality so blinds
Our senses that it seems less than a dream,
Yet we shall live to say 'Twice in a lifetime
We saw such nakedness that shame
Itself could not look on, and of all the feelings,
Hate, anger, justice, vengeance, violence, –
Horror alone remained, its organ voice
Searching us with a sickening clarity.'
And now the word comes in of those two cities
With all their living burden
Blown to the wind by power
Unused except by God at the creation, –
Atomised in the flash of an eye.
Who else but God or the instrument of God
Has power to pass such sentence?
Here the road forks, to survival or extinction,
And I hold my tongue through the awful silence,
For if God had nothing to do with it,
Extinction is the least price man can pay.

Edward Lowbury

[1] The day after the second Atomic Bomb which was dropped on Nagasaki

— The Meadow —

Reaching for a book I am reminded –
a spark illuminates a picture.
A meadow like a summer frock,
the sky a blue saucer,
the wind my mother's hand
and the sun
sketching lines of grass
on my outstretched arm.

An arm that gained full strength in Italy,
killed ruthlessly
beneath the shadow of an olive branch.

Now it reaches for a book
and I wonder about the meadow
and what went wrong.

Michael Armstrong

— Polliciti Meliora[1] —

As one who, gazing at a vista
  Of beauty, sees the clouds close in,
And turns his back in sorrow, hearing
  The thunderclouds begin,

So we, whose life was all before us,
  Our hearts with sunlight filled,
Left in the hills our books and flowers,
  Descended, and were killed.

Write on the stones no words of sadness –
  Only the gladness due,
That we, who asked the most of living,
  Knew how to give it too.

Frank Thompson

The poet was shot two years later whilst in Bulgaria on a special mission.

[1] 'Having promised better things.' (Latin)

Using this Anthology in the Classroom

Before reading

Although the aim of this anthology is to help students obtain a deeper understanding and appreciation of the poetry of World War Two, experience has shown that the reading of most poems dealing with the war (particularly if the poems are being read in the sections suggested here) can usefully be prefaced by providing students with opportunities to think about the area which each section covers. For example, before reading the poems about the period 'From 1939 to Dunkirk', students can ask their grandparents or older relations about their memories of the war's beginnings. What do they remember about the preparations for war – sandbags, gas-masks, the blackout? How did schools cope with air raids? What forces did grandparents serve in? Photographs and souvenirs, even old ration books, could form part of a classroom display, and students encouraged to make tape-recordings of their interviews with eye-witnesses. It might even be possible to invite a survivor from Dunkirk to give a talk to the whole class. Teachers could organise visits to museums within access of their school, e.g. the Imperial War Museum in London, Eden Camp in Yorkshire, the Tank Museum in Bovington, Dorset.

Exploring initial responses

Initial responses to a first reading of a poem may be explored individually, in pairs or in small groups. Some possibilities on first engaging with a particular poem might include:

- Read the poem and jot down first impressions. Work in pairs to compare notes.

- List images they find most striking and/or lines which particularly appeal to them.

- Use a cloze type procedure, with small groups. Delete certain words from a poem and ask students to suggest what words might best fill the gaps. This encourages students to focus on the author's style and vocabulary, and to understand how *precisely* a writer chooses his words. E.g. 'Cairo Jag' by Keith Douglas (p. 44) – deleting the metaphors and similes from the last verse and discussing possible replacements can reveal most effectively the force of Douglas' imagery.

• Sequencing helps students to focus on how a poem is constructed. A poem may be cut up into individual segments or stanzas and students asked to place the sections into what they consider to be the correct sequence. E.g. 'Rhine Jump, 1944' (p. 111) and 'Coming into the Clyde' (p. 97) – can be treated in this way.

• Withholding the title of a poem and inviting students to suggest a possible title is a way of helping to focus attention on the overall meaning of a poem. E.g. 'Night Preceding Battle' (p. 40) and 'Combat Report' (p. 89).

• Ask groups to formulate their own questions about a poem – What difficulties do they want explaining? – which can then be put to the whole class when groups come together to share their experiences.

Deepening and extending understanding

Further activities can be related to helping students to deepen and extend their responses:

• Rework a poem in another form, as a newspaper item or short story, and consider the difference between what they have written and the form of the original poem. E.g. 'Recce in Bocage Country' (p. 106).

• Write the imaginary diary entry of one of the characters mentioned in a poem, to reflect his or her reaction to events. E.g. what kind of day might one of the women described in 'Italian Road' (p. 78) have experienced?

• Write a letter from a character in a poem to a person outside the text. E.g. what kind of letter might the girl described in 'The Shelter' (p. 62) have written home to her parents about her experiences?

• Full class discussion to share feelings, ideas and unresolved questions about a poem. Such a discussion might examine some of the following areas:
What does the poem say to you?
How does the poet use language, rhythm and/or style to convey mood and meaning?
Compare the surface meaning of a poem with its implied sub-text.
Does the poem work for *you*?

• Written essays or other relevant pieces of writing suitable for coursework folders.

Further activities

The pleasure of sharing responses to poetry by class discussion can be complemented and enhanced by other activities which encourage a range of responses:

- Students work in groups to compile an anthology of their favourite poems, suitably illustrated with drawings, maps and photographs, giving reasons for their choices, and with lines, phrases or verses picked out for special comment.

- Performance of a poem or poems by small groups for the rest of the class. Students can tackle this in different ways in order to heighten dramatic effect:
  the use of different voices to interpret different poems;
  using sound effects such as tape recordings of explosions, sirens, music;
  suggest gestures, *tableaux*, movements to accompany a poem.
  E.g. poems such as F. A. Horn's 'Reveille–1943' (p. 65) can form the basis for extended improvisations – as students work to create the sense, not only of the billet coming to life in the morning, but of the world elsewhere which is suggested by the poem.

- The best response to a poem is often for students to try to write their own poems. Writing a parody or imitation of poems or specific forms is a useful way of starting. E.g. compare I. G. Fletcher's blank verse imitation (p. 73) with Tennyson's original 'Morte d'Arthur'.
  Henry Reed's 'Lessons of the War' (p. 27) can be used as a starting point for parodies, such as 'The school fire drill'.
  Students can be asked to write verse replies to poems. E.g. Use Elsie Cawser's 'Salvage Song' as a model for a reply from a Hurricane pilot writing to thank her for the salvage he is now flying!

The best poems come from students' immersion in reading poetry, but show evidence of a response to it by demonstrating a freshness and originality of their own. As with all writing, but probably even more critically with poetry writing, students should be encouraged to draft and redraft their work.

Although the poems in this anthology are arranged in groups which cover the different phases of World War Two, teachers may feel that they can make better connections between particular poems and the needs of their students. Teachers should not feel bound by the pattern chosen by the editors and be able to group and teach poems on lines which seem more appropriate for their purposes.

Use can also be made of the *Oasis* tape (C-90 cassette) and video (details of which can be found on page x).

The Activities which follow suggest more detailed work activities which students may pursue.

Activities

1. From 1939 to Dunkirk

• 'Epitaph on a New Army' and *'Polliciti Meliora'* (the first and the last poems in the anthology) are two poems in which writers try to describe reasons for taking part in the war and possibly being killed. Can you say which of the two poems you prefer and give reasons for your choice?

• In 'All Day It Has Rained', Alun Lewis describes a number of soldiers waiting to go off to the war. Write a description of the way you have seen people behave while waiting for something unpleasant to happen (e.g. in a dentist's waiting room).

• After you have read 'The Bofors AA Gun', pick out two other poems from this section and *War in the Air* which seem to you to give pictures of the machinery of war, and then say how the poems give such vivid pictures. You may particularly wish to consider the words used by the poets.

• Compare 'Before the First Parachute Descent' with 'Parachute Jump' in Section 7. What are the differences between the two poems? Which of them gives a better picture of the parachutist's feelings?

2. The Middle East

• 'Advice for a Journey' uses metaphors about a journey to describe preparations for war. Select three metaphors that seem particularly effective, and say what they suggest to you.

• After reading 'It's Always Mealtime', try to write a poem about school-dinners, following the same pattern of rhymed couplets as in the original.

• Read 'The Taking of the Koppie' carefully. Write a short prose account of the incident described by the young man. Then write a paragraph about the poet's feelings about the young man and his story.

• What were the events behind 'Beyond the Wire'? Write a prose account of what you think happened, and then compare it with the poem's brief description.

• After reading 'Elegy for an 88 Gunner', think about the German soldier and his girl friend Steffi. *Either* write a letter from him sent to Steffi the day before the battle, *or* write a letter from Steffi to him, on hearing that he might be going into battle.

- 'Night Preceding Battle' is the poetic expression of a man's thoughts and feelings. Compare it with other 'poems of conscience' in this anthology, for example 'My Hands' by Mary Harrison on page 84. What do they tell of the attitude of those who served and believed that the war was necessary?

- In 'Hospital Afternoon' Hamish Henderson uses a number of metaphors and similes to describe the situation and his feelings. Pick out *three* images which seem successful to you, and *one* which seems less successful. Why do you think it works less well?

- After you have read 'Desert Conflict', try to imagine the African soldier who wrote it. Write a story describing how he came to be fighting in the war and his feelings, and those of his family, on leaving home for the war front.

3.   The Home Front

- 'Behind the Screens' was written by a nurse for a soldier who is separated from the rest of the hospital ward by screens. Suggest either a) a group dramatisation of the scene, or b) draft notes on how it might be dramatised to bring out the contrast between the activities and the noise of the rest of the ward and the peace behind the screens.

- Having read 'Steel Cathedrals', either a) make a sketch of a war-time railway station illustrating any of the word-pictures in the poem, or b) in your own words, write a prose version of the poem as though you were writing an article for a magazine.

- 'Night Piece for You' is an early version of a poem by Geoffrey Matthews which has also been published under the title of 'Nocturne'. This runs:

> Smoke from the municipal dump blows sleepily over
> Newmarket; racehorses on the heath are ridden down
> To breathy paddocks, and the last lights are all covered.
> Evening in Air Force blue leans at the end of the town.
>
> Lovers in slacks and battledress on their physical errands
> Loiter past, unfocus, sombre are no longer seen.
> Thigh-deep already in shadows the cinemas stand
> Posing, where the dun staff-cars founder like plasticine.
>
> Far out along the sea-coloured coasts of Norfolk,
> From ruts and estuaries, the searchlights raise their arms
> Palms uppermost, pressing up against the cloud-pack,
> Withholding the heavy fire from camp and farm.

Two factory-chimneys a long way off fume and labour,
Tops black against duck's-egg, trunks in cinnamon.
A concert of travelling stars. Bomber after bomber
Steps overland to rehearse the destiny of man.

In the first verse of 'Nocturne' you will notice that the poet prefers to use 'leans' instead of 'philanders'. Make a list of the changes Geoffrey Matthews has made to the poem. Suggest why you think he might have made these changes.

- What is it like to be in an air-raid? Ask your grandparents or older friends what it feels like and what they did. Collect pictures of bombed buildings, and then try to write a poem about what you imagine it would feel like if a bomb fell near your house.

4. The Mediterranean and Italy

- 'The White Conscript and the Black Conscript' contains an imaginary dialogue between a white and a black soldier fighting on the same side. What is the white man trying to tell the black man? Rewrite the poem as a prose dialogue – as though it were an extract from a play – in which the two men discuss their differences and their similarities.

- Read 'The Soldiers at Lauro' carefully. Why does the poet refer to 'crosses' and 'helmets' in the last two lines? Write a paraphrase of the poem in continuous prose. What effect does the poetic version achieve with its use of rhyme and rhythm?

- After you have read 'Cassino', pick out two other poems from Sections 2, 4 or 7 which give pictures of land battles. Select words and phrases from each poem which seem to you to convey the sensations of battle most effectively.

- 'Burial Party' describes the tragi-comedy which arose from trying to move an Italian officer's body. Can you find any other poems which show how situations in wartime sometimes bring out an unexpected sense of humour? Can you describe a situation in which you, or someone you know, have giggled at a very serious moment?

5. War in the Air

- After you have read 'Death of a Man of Kent', try to write a four-line epitaph in memory of the dead pilot.

- Read 'To a German Airman' carefully. What does the poem tell you of the attitude of the poet to the enemy? [Refer also to the poet's biography on page 155 for his war record.]

- Read 'Heil Hamburg, Forty One' carefully. See if you can identify the different moods of the poem as it changes every few lines from the opening paragraph to the last line. Write down the key words that you think show the changes of mood.

- After reading 'When He Is Flying', pick out two other poems which deal with love and relationships in wartime. (You will find examples in Sections 2, 6, 7 and 10.) Say which one of the three you prefer, and select words or phrases which particularly appeal to you.

- Read 'Luck' carefully. What does it tell us about the poet's attitude to war? For many servicemen and women it has become *the* poem of war. Why do you think this is?

6.   War at Sea

- Read 'Convoy at Night' carefully. Then make a sketch of any line or image in the poem which conveys a powerful picture to you.

- Read 'Leaving the Med.' carefully. Try to cut the poem down from its present length by reducing each verse to what you consider to be its most important lines. What is the contrast the poet is describing between journeys in verses 1, 2, and 4, and in verse 3? Write a sentence in your own words which sums up what you think the poet means by the last two verses.

- After reading 'Still No Letter', write a letter to the sailor on his mine-sweeper, explaining the (war-time) reasons for your delay in writing.

7.   War in North West Europe: From Normandy to Berlin

- Read 'Poor Dead Panzer' carefully. What do you think the significance of the references to the pistol is in verses 2 and 3? Write a story about the events in the day which led up to the action described in the poem.

- After you have read 'Love Letters of the Dead' look at 'Elegy for an 88 Gunner' (Section 2) and 'The Enemy Dead' (Section 8). Do you think the sergeant was right to be angry with the poet? Working with another student, argue out the *pros* and *cons* of the Intelligence Briefing.

- 'The Weeping Beeches of Sonnenberg' is one of the few poems in the *Oasis* series written in retrospect. (Each year the veterans of Arnhem go back on a pilgrimage and pick up the fallen leaves of Sonnenberg.) What moods does the poet express in the first two verses of the poem? Explain how the poet's feelings have changed by the ending of the poem. Can you suggest an alternative title for the poem which describes this change of mood?

8.   South East Asia and the Pacific

• After you have read 'Bengal Summer', find two other poems from this section about places, one appreciative and one critical. Select lines from the poem you like most that give a vivid impression of the place.

• Find out how Singapore was captured by the Japanese in 1942, and then read 'The Fortress of the East' carefully. Write a paragraph describing the kind of person who might have spoken the first ten lines of the poem.

• Read the extract from 'The Jungle' by Alun Lewis. It is not an easy poem to understand quickly, so make a list of questions about the poem which you would like answered to make the poem easier for you to understand. Discuss these questions and possible answers with each other in groups.

• Read 'Askari Song: Airdrop' carefully. What is the irony which the Nyasaland soldiers describe in verses 2 and 3? How is the poem similar to and different from 'Desert Conflict' by Calvin Makabo (Section 2)?

9.   Behind the Wire

• Select one or two lines from each verse-paragraph of 'Midwinter' which seem to summarise the poet's feelings in the Italian prison-camp. Are there any one or two lines which sum up the whole poem for you?

• 'Oflag Night Piece, Colditz' is a sonnet, a poetic form in which the last six lines often contain an idea or a feeling in sharp contrast to the first eight lines. What is the paradoxical contrast suggested by this poem? 'Counter Battery Fire' (Section 4) and 'War Graves' (Section 10) are also sonnets built upon contrasts. In small groups discuss these sonnets – which of the three do *you* think conveys the sense of contrast most effectively?

• Read 'Last Post' carefully. Then by commenting upon the poet's choice of particular words and use of rhythms, say how he suggests the contrast between the noise and the quiet of the prison-camp.

• Write what you think is the significance of the five wheat grains in 'Day of Liberation, Bergen–Belsen, May 1945'. What does the poem tell you about the struggle to survive? Now look at the photograph and the diary entry. What do they tell you? Describe your reactions to each.

10.   Aftermath

• How does the position of the trucks indicate that peace has come in 'Italy to Austria'? Read the poem again carefully, and then write a poem about the news of the ending of the war in Britain. If you like, you can begin the poem 'We knew that peace had come . . .'

- Discuss 'War Graves'. What do you think the poet means when he says 'We are all guilty'? Can you think of ways people who survived the war might be said to have paid for it afterwards?

- After reading 'August 10th, 1945 – The Day After', select two or three lines which seem to you particularly striking or interesting. Write down the questions you would like answered in order to help you to understand the poem better. Discuss the questions and possible answers with each other in groups.

- 'Let's Go Back' and 'Release Group Blues' describe the difficulties two servicemen experienced when they began to return to civilian life. Compare the two poems and discuss which you think describes the more serious problem. Working in pairs, argue the points of view of the two men.

- 'Budget for Romance' describes the difficulties a servicewoman anticipated before returning to civilian life. Say what you think she thought the main problem might be, and why she had not found this difficulty earlier. What other problems do you think servicewomen might have found on returning to civilian life after the war?

General activities

- Many of the poems in this anthology are about the horrors of war. Select two poems which have made you most aware of its horrors, and write about how these poems make an impact upon you.

- If you were asked by a friend to recommend one poem about World War Two from this anthology, which poem would you suggest and why? You may wish to write about the excitement and the feeling, the atmosphere, the rhythms and the language used in the poem you choose.

- Working in groups, select your five favourite poems from the anthology. Discuss how each poem is to be read aloud and by whom, and whether the use of sound effects may be useful or not. Then tape record your group's presentation of the poems, and play it to another class, or to an audience of parents or older people who lived through World War Two.

- Write a poem about people in war or any aspect of war that concerns you.

- From the biographies on page 153 list the poets killed in action. Note the activities on which they were engaged. Then, select two or three of the poets and read their poems again. What do you learn from the biographical details and the poems about the poets and their attitudes to the war?

- Examine carefully the illustrations and photographs used in this collection, and select one which seems to you to add most to your understanding and appreciation of a particular poem. Give reasons, and then discuss your choice with each other in groups.

Biographies

†*Died in World War Two*

The editors have compiled basic biographies of the poets, where the information was available.

†**Drummond ALLISON** [p. 79]: Born 1921, Caterham, Surrey. Educated Bishop's Stortford and Queen's College, Oxford. Sandhurst 1942. East Surrey Regiment. Killed on the Garigliano, Italy, 2 December 1943.

'ALMENDRO' [p. 40]: Denis Saunders. South African Air Force, poet and joint-founder of *Oasis* in Cairo, 1942. Today a homoeopathic doctor in Randburg.

Michael ARMSTRONG [p. 143]: Born 1923, Newcastle-upon-Tyne. Educated Sedbergh. Army 1942–47, KSLI Italy. Later librarian. Tended the gorillas in Gerald Durrell's Zoo, Channel Islands.

John BAYLISS [p. 86]: Born 1919, Gloucestershire. Educated Latymer Upper and St. Catherine's College, Cambridge. Flight lieutenant in RAF. Co-editor with Alex Comfort of *New Road, 1943–44*. Post-war, publishing and Civil Service.

Jack BEVAN [p. 71]: Born 1920. Educated Cambridge University. Commissioned Royal Artillery 1943, served in Italy. Post-war teacher, poet and translator. Poems in *My Sad Pharaohs* (Routledge and Kegan Paul).

D. Van den BOGAERDE [p. 61]: Born 1921. University College School and Allen Glen's School. Served in Europe and Far east, Queen's Royal Regiment. Known as film actor Dirk Bogarde and author of many books, including *A Postillion Struck by Lightning* (Chatto and Windus).

Angela BOLTON [p. 118]: Born Preston 1918. Educated Winckley Square Convent School. Nursed in Burma, 14th Army. Post-war nursing sister Oxford. Wrote *The Maturing Sun* (Imperial War Museum).

Basil G. BONALLACK [p. 32]: Born 1907. Educated Mill Hill School and Clare College, Cambridge. Honourable Artillery Company at Dunkirk. The 'Dunkirk' poem was begun in France 1940 and completed on the Anzio beach-head 1944.

John E. BROOKES [p. 72]: Worked his passage from Liverpool to Australia pre-war. Private with 2/5 Bn Australian Infantry Force (AIF) 1940–1945. POW Salonika. Today lives at Castle Cary, Somerset. Writer, poet.

John BUXTON [p. 31]: Born 1912, Cheshire. Malvern and New College, Oxford. A pre-war poet, served in No. 1 Independent Company. Prisoner, Norway, 1940. Interned in Oflag VII.

Elsie CAWSER [p. 60]: Born 1915, Staffordshire. During the war technician, Dairy Laboratory. Lives in Derbyshire.

Louis CHALLONER [p. 52]: Born 1911, Blackpool. Preston Grammar School and University College, Southampton. Western Desert from Alamein to Algiers. Post-war head teacher at Newham. Oasis Trust Archivist.

David Stafford CLARK [p. 85]: DPM, FRCP, FRC. Psych. Born 1915. Educated Felsted School, University of London, Guy's Hospital. RAFVR 1939–45, became medical parachutist. Twice mentioned in despatches.

Les CLEVELAND [p. 74]: 2nd New Zealand Expeditionary Force, Pacific, Egypt, Italy, where wounded. Published The Iron Hand (poetry). Later Reader in Political Science, Victoria University, Wellington, New Zealand.

J. M. COLLARD [p. 86]: Served in the Middle East. A historian, lives at Gerrards Cross, Bucks.

Joy CORFIELD [p. 60, 141]: Born 1925, Manchester. Special Wireless Operator, then driver in Germany. Disabled by polio 1950.

Michael CROFT, OBE [p. 101]: Burnage Grammar School. RAF 1940–41, Royal Navy 1942–46. Post-war Keble College, Oxford and taught at Alleyn's School. Founded the National Youth Theatre. Died 1986.

John CROMER, OBE [p. 37]: Major. Middle East in Intelligence. Co-founder Salamander Society, Cairo. Post-war legal profession. Head of Consumer Protection EEC.

Dan DAVIN, CBE [p. 56]: Born New Zealand, Rhodes Scholar Oxford. Platoon Commander 23rd NZ Battalion Greece. Wounded Crete. Official NZ historian. Served at Cassino. Short story writer and novelist. Post-war Oxford University Press. Died 1990.

Erik DE MAUNY [p. 69]: Born 1920 London. Victoria University College, New Zealand and University of London. NZ Expeditionary Force, Pacific, Middle East and Italy. Post-war BBC foreign correspondent.

†Keith DOUGLAS [p. 44, 45, 46]: Born 1920 Tunbridge Wells. Christ's Hospital and Merton College, Oxford. Poet pre-war. Derbyshire Yeomanry, Captain, against orders fought at El Alamein. Killed Normandy, June 1944. His poems in this book are his originals from Editions Poetry London, as in all the Oasis anthologies. His prose account of El Alamein with his poems in Alamein to Zem Zem (Editions Poetry London).

Norman Maxwell DUNN [p. 139]: Born Sydney, Australia 1916. An accountant, commissioned under the Empire Air Training Scheme. Flew with 258 Hurricane Fighter Squadron. POW Germany four years. Lives in New South Wales.

John DURNFORD [p. 132]: Born Edinburgh 1920. Educated Sherborne and Trinity Hall, Cambridge. Commissioned Royal Artillery, India and Malaya. Captured at fall of Singapore 1942. Prisoner of war Siam until 1945. Post-war sales representative and wrote Branch Line to Burma (1988).

Gavin EWART [p. 28]: Born 1916. Wellington and Christ's College, Cambridge. Worked in advertising. Royal Artillery Officer, North Africa and Italy. Post-war an established poet. Lives in London.

Olivia FITZROY [p. 88]: Born 1921, daughter of Viscount Daventry. WRNS Direction Officer 1944, Ceylon. Post-war wrote Wagons and Horses (1955). Died 1969.

Ian FLETCHER [p. 140]: Born 1922 London. Served in Middle East. Poetry includes *Orisons* and *Twenty One Poems*. Professor of English at Arizona University and before at Reading University. Oasis Trust Editor. Died 1988.

Ivor George FLETCHER [p. 73]: Born 1920 Stafford. Lieutenant, Staffordshire Regiment. North Africa. Severely wounded 1943. Post-war a teacher, lives in Surrey.

G. S. FRASER [p. 42]: Born 1915. MA St Andrews. Trainee journalist Aberdeen Press & Journal. Warrant Officer Class 2 Army Middle East, Ministry of Information. Post-war lecturer Japan and Leicester University. A Salamander Oasis Trust founder. Died 1980.

Roy FULLER, CBE [pp. 77, 96]: Born 1912. St Paul's School. Navy, first as ordinary seaman, then officer Fleet Air Arm. Poetry includes *The Middle of a War* (1942) and *Epitaphs and Orations* (1949). Awarded the Queen's Medal for Poetry 1970 and elected Professor of Poetry at Oxford University 1968–73. Died 1991.

Brian GALLIE [p. 82]: Royal Navy Captain, served in the Mediterranean and awarded the DSC. Died 1982 Portugal.

Wilfrid GIBSON [p. 62]: Born Hexham, Northumberland 1880. Also poet of World War One. Published *The Searchlights* (contains 'The Shelter') 1943. Died 1962.

E. F. GOSLING [p. 40]: Yeomanry Regiment Lieutenant Colonel. Served in Middle East.

Grace GRIFFITHS [p. 65]: Born Devon 1921. Crediton High School. ATS (Royal Signals). Post-war librarian.

Bernard GUTTERIDGE [p. 123]: Born 1916 Southampton. Cranleigh School. Combined Ops and with 36th Division Burma (with Alun Lewis). A Major. Advertising career post-war. Died 1985.

Michael HAMBURGER [p. 31]: MBE. Born 1924 Berlin. Westminster and Christ Church College, Oxford. Army 1943–47. Visiting Professor, Universities of Carolina and Boston; translator.

Norman HAMPSON [p. 100]: Born 1922. Manchester Grammar School and University College, Oxford. Ordinary Seaman HMS *Carnation* and Sub-Lieutenant HMS *Easton*, escorting convoys in Eastern Mediterranean. Post-war Professor of History, York.

Melville HARDIMENT [p. 108]: Regular Army sergeant 2nd East Yorks Regiment, landed in Normandy D-Day, wounded Toufreville, east of Caen, 41 days later.

Mary HARRISON [p. 84]: Born Smalley, Derbyshire 1921. WAAF trained as Model Maker RAF Medmenham, Bucks, made models for the Dam raids, Ploesti Oil Fields and Cologne, which inspired the poem. Lives in Nottinghamshire.

Gwenyth HAYES [p. 68]: Middle East First New Zealand Voluntary Aid Detachment from January 1942. Later private secretary to officer commanding 2nd New Zealand General Hospital at Kantara in Egypt then Italy. Twice mentioned in despatches.

Hamish HENDERSON [p. 51]: Born Perthshire 1919. Dulwich College and Downing College, Cambridge. Intelligence Officer 51st Highland Division at Alamein, Tunisia, Sicily and at Anzio. Liaison Officer with Italian partisans. Post-war Research Fellow in School of Scottish Studies.

John Buxton HILTON [p. 109]: Born 1921 Buxton. Cambridge University. Sergeant Intelligence Corps, mentioned in despatches. Post-war teacher and an HMI before becoming a crime writer. Died 1986.

Geoffrey HOLLOWAY [p. 111]: Born Birmingham 1918. Alsop High School, Liverpool. Royal Army Medical Corps 6th Airborne Division, North West Europe. Post-war social work at Cumbria.

F. A. HORN [pp. 65, 140]: Born Bradford 1906. Bradford College of Art. Royal Army Ordnance Corps. Post-war advertising and publicity. Died 1975.

Jim HOVELL [p. 109]: Born North London 1922. Highgate School. Commissioned Royal Armoured Corps North West Europe. Post-war advertising and public relations.

P. A. HYATT [p. 112]: Airborne Division North West Europe, including Arnhem/Oosterbruch 1944. Military Medal. Died Western Australia 1983.

John S. INGRAM [p. 26]: Born Willesden 1915. Perse School, Cambridge. Commissioned 1943, served in Gibraltar. Playwright. Founded Harrow Theatre Group.

Robin IVY [p. 137]: Born 1919. Lance-corporal, North Africa, Italy and Austria. Post-war teacher but retired early to write poetry.

†**John JARMAIN** [p. 53]: Captain Anti-tank Unit 51st Highland Division. Served chiefly Western Desert. Killed June 1944 Normandy by mortar bomb whilst on recce: could have left it to others but overwhelming sense of duty.

Norman G. JONES [p. 81]: Born Ebbw Vale 1921. Ebbw Vale County School. RAF wireless operator. Post-war safety officer British Steel.

†**Sidney KEYES** [p. 36]: Born Dartford 1922. Tonbridge and Queen's College, Oxford. Lieutenant Queen's Own Royal West Kent Regiment. North Africa. Killed on patrol Tunisia April 1943. Talented schoolboy poet, posthumously awarded the Hawthornden Prize for The Iron Laurel (1942) and The Cruel Solstice (1943).

Uys KRIGE [pp. 50, 126]: Born Swellendam, South Africa, 1910. University of Stellenbosch. War correspondent Egypt. Prisoner-of-war Italy, described in his autobiography The Way Out, 1946. South Africa's leading poet of World War Two. Died 1987.

†**Alun LEWIS** [pp. 30, 116]: Born 1915 Aberdare. Cowbridge Grammar School and University College of Wales. A teacher, wrote pre-war. Enlisted 1940 Lieutenant South Wales Borderers. Killed Arakan Front, Burma, 5 March 1944. Poetry includes Raider's Dawn (1942) and Ha! Ha! among the Trumpets (1945). Collected Stories published by Seren Books 1991.

Edward LOWBURY [p. 142]: Born 1913 St Paul's School and University College Oxford. Specialist in Pathology. Royal Army Medical Corps 1943–47. Post-war Professor, Aston University.

Redmond MACDONOGH [p. 83]: Born 1915. St Aloysius College, Highgate and London University. Commissioned 1937. Pilot No. 21 and 101 Squadrons. Wrote plays for BBC. Died 1986.

Somhairle MACGILL-EAIN (Sorley MACLEAN) [p. 48]: Born 1911 Isle of Raasay. Edinburgh University. Signal Corps in the Desert. Wounded at Alamein. Post-war teacher writer and leading Gaelic poet.

†**Calvin MAKABO** [p. 55]: Sergeant 1946 Company AAPC (Basuto), Western Desert. Drowned west of Tripoli 1943. [Translation of the poem by Sgt Alexander Qoboshane]

John MANIFOLD [p. 43]: Born 1915. Geelong Grammar School and Jesus College, Cambridge. British Army West Africa and Europe. Returned to Queensand, Australia in 1949.

Geoffrey MATTHEWS [p. 64]: Born 1920. Kingswood School, Bath and Corpus Christi College, Oxford. Royal Signals Middle East. Post-war taught at Leeds and Reading Universities. Died 1984.

Charles McCAUSLAND [pp. 54, 124]: Born New South Wales, Australia 1910. Glen Innes High School and Sydney University. Australian Infantry Force Egypt, Lebanon and Libya and New Guinea. Post-war teacher NSW, visiting Associate Professor, University of Calgary, Alberta, later Vice-Principal Bathurst Teachers College, NSW.

Dennis McHARRIE, OBE [p. 89]: Flight Lieutenant RAF in the Desert, later reaching rank of Wing Commander. Lives at Blackpool, Lancs.

Colin McINTYRE [p. 107]: Born Argentina 1927. Commissioned Black Watch. Company Commander, Lovat Scouts, Greece and Palestine. Post-war BBC journalist, became editor of CEEFAX.

Alexander McKEE [p. 110]: Born Ipswich 1918. St Helen's College, Southsea. London Scottish and Gordon Highlanders, Normandy 1944. Post-war writer and radio producer. In Mary Rose project.

Spike MILLIGAN [p. 76]: Born India 1918. Bombadier Royal Artillery North Africa and Italy. Post-war radio and TV comedian and scriptwriter especially *The Goon Show*. Books include *Silly Verse for Kids* (1970) and *Monty: His Part In My Victory* (1978).

Norman T. MORRIS [p. 38]: Born 1912

Cheshire. Educated Lancaster Royal Grammar School. 50th Royal Tank Regiment Western Desert, Italy and Greece. Post-war headmaster at a London school. College lecturer and examiner.

William E. MORRIS [p. 98]: New Zealand Expeditionary Force, Middle East and Italy. NCO on railways in Desert Construction Unit. Poems translated into Hindi and Russian. Lives at Bay of Plenty, NZ.

Eric A. OXLEY [p. 120]: Born Sydney, Australia 1914. Sydney High School and Sydney University. Commissioned 1st Australian Armoured Regiment. A community pharmacist, lives in New South Wales.

John PUDNEY [p. 89]: Born 1909. Gresham School in Norfolk. Journalist, became Squadron Leader, RAF. Wrote many 'Air Poems' such as 'For Johnny' in *Dispersal Point* (1942) and *South of Forty* (1943). Post-war full-time writer. Died 1977.

Frederick RACKSTRAW [p. 132]: Born Aylesbury 1908. Royal Corps of Signals Malaya Command 1941–42. Taken prisoner-of-war at Singapore. Worked on Thailand Burma Railway, 1943–45. Post-war Pearl Assurance Company. Died 1980.

Henry REED [p. 27]: Born 1914. Birmingham University. Journalist pre-war, served in Royal Army Ordnance Corps, then Foreign Office. War poems in *The Map of Verona* (1945). Post-war BBC. Died 1986.

†George S. RICHARDSON [p. 118]: Born Ponteland, Northumberland 1914. Berwick Grammar School and Durham University. Joined RAF 1937, posted Singapore. Shot down by Japanese Zero

fighters off Johore, Malaya 1942. Mentioned in despatches.

John RIMINGTON [p. 47]: Born 1918. Canford School, Dorset. Journalist pre-war. RASC, driving a tank transporter in the Desert. Briefly captured by the Germans. Lost many manuscripts. Post-war advertising and marketing. Died 1977.

Michael RIVIERE [p. 128]: Born 1919. Commissioned Sherwood Rangers Yeomanry. Taken prisoner Crete 1941. After his second escape from Eichstatt, Bavaria, 1943, sent to Colditz (Oflag IV C). Mentioned in despatches.

R. M. ROBERTS [p. 78]: Born Burnley 1909. Royal Corps of Signals Western Desert and Italy. Post-war built up furniture business in Burnley.

Alan ROOK [p. 58]: Born 1909. Uppingham School and Oxford University. Royal Artillery, Dunkirk, became Major 6th AA Division, invalided out. War poetry in *Soldiers, This Solitude* (1942) and *These Are My Comrades* (1943).

Alan ROSS [p. 95]: Born 1922. Haileybury and St John's College, Oxford. Joined Royal Navy as Ordinary Seaman on convoys to Russia. Later Intelligence Officer with Destroyer Flotilla. Post-war editor of *London Magazine*. Wrote *Something of the Sea* (1954).

Roger ROTHWELL [p. 130]: Lieutenant 1st Battalion Middlesex Regiment. Prisoner-of-war, Hong Kong. Poems written in prison camp hospital. Post-war headmaster of Tideway School, Newhaven, Sussex.

Peter RUSSELL [p. 120]: Born Bristol 1921. Indian Army Burma and Malaya. Post-war edited *Literary Review* 1976–77, poet in residence Dundee University and University of Victoria, British Columbia.

George SHEPPERSON [p. 122]: Born Peterborough 1922. King's School, Peterborough and St John's College, Cambridge. Commissioned Northamptonshire Regiment. Seconded to King's African Rifles. Nyasaland Battalion, East Africa, India and Burma. Post-war university teacher and Professor of Commonwealth and American History, Edinburgh University.

Kenneth SLESSOR [p. 102]: Born 1901, Orange, NSW. Journalist. Australian Official War Correspondent Greece, Middle East, New Guinea. Post-war writer, editor. Commonwealth Literary Fund Advisory Board, National Literature Board of Review. Died Sydney 1971.

Martin SOUTHALL [p. 79]: Born Aston, Birmingham 1924. Commissioned Queen's Royal Regiment. Italy and Gold Coast, RWAFF. Post-war engineering firm. Poems in *Behind the Pale Horse* (1987).

†**Richard SPENDER** [p. 29]: Born Hereford 1921. King Edward VI School, Stratford-on-Avon. Won scholarship to Oxford 1940 but enlisted in London Irish Regiment. Volunteered for Parachute Regiment. March 1943 killed in Tunisia leading his men against German machine-gun positions. Poems in *Laughing Blood* (1942) and *Parachute Battalion* (1943).

Douglas STREET [p. 105]: Born 1915. Mother a Belgian artist. Hertford College, Oxford. TA Expeditionary Force at Dunkirk, liaison with Free French. SOE in Yugoslavia and Greece. Post-war Foreign Office.

†**Frank THOMPSON** [p. 143]: Born Darjeeling 1920. Winchester and New College, Oxford. Commissioned Royal Artillery 1940, Special Duties Western Desert and Sicily. Gifted linguist, parachuted into Balkans to work with the

Partisans. Captured and shot 1944, Sofia, Bulgaria.

Michael THWAITES [pp. 25, 97]: Born Brisbane, Australia 1915. Geelong Grammar School, Melbourne University and New College, Oxford. Royal Naval Volunteer Reserve 1939–45 trawlers and corvettes in Atlantic and North Sea. Lecturer Melbourne University 1950–70, Australian Intelligence 1971–76. Publications include *The Jervis Bay and Other Poems* (1943) and *Poems of War and Peace* (1966).

N. J. TRAPNELL [p. 39]: Served in the Western Desert. Poems also in *Return to Oasis* (1980).

Henry TREECE [p. 29]: Born Wednesbury, Staffordshire 1912. Wednesbury High School and Birmingham University. School teacher pre-war. RAF Intelligence. Post-war teaching and full-time writing. Co-edited *Air Force Poetry* with John Pudney in 1944. *Collected Poems* (1946). Novels include *Jason* (1961). Died 1966.

Donald E. VINCENT [p. 87]: Born 1923 Penarth, South Glamorganshire. Penarth County School. Flight-Sergeant Bomb-aimer RAF 1944–45. Post-war civil servant, farmer and sales representative.

John WALLER [p. 99]: Born Oxford 1917. Weymouth College and Worcester College, Oxford. Captain RASC Middle East 1941–46. Succeeded to Baronetcy 1954. Poet and novelist. *Fortunate Hamlet* (1941) and *The Merry Ghosts* (1946). Keats Prize for Poetry 1947. Elected Fellow of the Royal Society of Literature 1948.

John WARRY [p. 141]: Born 1916. Haileybury and Queen's College, Cambridge. Intelligence Corps and Army Education Corps. Post-war lecturer Alexandria University, Cyprus and senior lecturer RMA Sandhurst. Historical novels and short stories.

John WEDGE [p. 96]: Born London 1921. RNVR. Telegraphist on minesweeper *Norse*, later officer HMS *Worcester*. Post-war Barclays Bank.

Victor WEST [p. 138]: Born Clapham 1919. Simon Langton School, Canterbury. Lance-Corporal 1st Rangers KRRC. Prisoner Crete, escaped 1945 in Eastern Europe. Post-war taught, acted and painted. Published poetry anthology *The Horses of Falaise* (1975).

Jo WESTREN [p. 59]: Born Essex 1914. RAMC nurse attached to anti-aircraft command and Colchester Military Hospital. Poems in *Harvests* (1978).

Phillip WHITFIELD [p. 134]: Born Bombay 1918. Tettenhall College (Staffs). University College and Hospital. Captain RAMC. A medical examiner of Belsen victims. Post-war community medicine and paediatrics. Poems in *A Dram of Time* (1987).

Darrell WILKINSON [p. 98]: Born 1919. Epsom College and St Thomas's Hospital, London. Surgeon-Lieutenant RNVR. SOE Greece and Crete 1942–46. Post-war consultant dermatologist. Trust founder.

Kenneth WILSON [p. 92]: Born Hull 1916. Joined Royal Navy 1932. Petty Officer Telegraphist destroyers Atlantic and Malta convoys. Post-war teacher. Works include *The Abbeys of Yorkshire* and two books of poetry.

Peter YOUNG [p. 106]: Born Portsmouth 1920. Portsmouth Municipal College. Trooper Westminster Dragoons, later Sergeant in the Education Corps. Post-war teacher and educational books. Joint-author of *Dyslexia or Illiteracy*.

Acknowledgements for Poems and Photographs

All poems, aside from 'Beach Burial' by Kenneth Slessor, have been published in previous *Oasis* anthologies, where the copyright and permissions have been duly acknowledged.

However, the Trust has endeavoured once again to contact all poets and families and gratefully acknowledges specific permissions from:

Collins Angus & Robertson, Australia for permission to reprint 'Beach Burial' by Kenneth Slessor; Octopus Publishing Group Library for 'The White Conscript and the Black Conscript' and 'Royal Naval Air Station' by Roy Fuller; The Rt. Hon. A. Jessel for 'When He is Flying' by Olivia Fitzroy; Michael Thwaites 'Epitaph on a New army'; John S. Ingram 'Selection Board'; Gavin Ewart 'The Bofors AA GUN'; Michael Hamburger 'Sentry Duty'; John Buxton 'The Tarn'; B.G. Bonallack 'Dunkirk' (extract); Louis Challoner 'Alternative'; John Cromer 'Beyond the Wire'; Almendro (Dr Denis Saunders) 'Night Preceding Battle'; Somhairle Macgill-eain (Sorley MacLean) 'Latha Foghair/An Autumn Day'; Hamish Henderson 'Hospital Afternoon'; N.J. Trapnell 'Lament of a Desert Rat'; Jo Westren 'Behind the Screens'; Elsie Cawser 'The Salvage Song (or The Housewife's Dream)'; Geoffrey Matthews (from Mrs Matthews) 'Night Piece for You'; Grace Griffiths 'Doodlebugs'; I.G. Fletcher (from Mrs Fletcher) 'Morte d'Arthur'; Gwenyth Hayes 'This Italy'; J. Bevan 'Counter-Battery Fire'; Spike Milligan 'The Soldiers at Lauro'; Les Cleveland 'Cassino' (extract); J.E. Brookes 'Burial Party'; R.M. Roberts 'Italian Road'; Erik de Mauny 'Morning After Battle'; Martin Southall 'May-1945'; J.M. Collard 'Death of a Man of Kent'; Brian Gallie (from Mrs Gallie) 'To a German Airman'; Mary Harrison 'My Hands'; Donald E. Vincent 'Silly Sort of Past-Time'; Dennis McHarrie 'Luck'; John Wedge 'Still No Letter'; Michael Thwaites 'Coming into the Clyde'; Norman Hampson 'Assault Convoy'; Darrell Wilkinson 'Drifting a Sea'; Peter Young 'Recce in Bocage Country'; Jim Hovell 'Landscape with Tanks'; Douglas Street 'Love Letters of the Dead'; Geoffrey Holloway 'Rhine Jump, 1944'; Alexander McKee 'The Question'; Angela Bolton 'Bengal Summer'; Eric A. Oxley 'Morobe'; Charles McCausland 'Dead Japanese'; Michael Riviere 'Oflag Night Piece, Colditz'; John Durnford 'Lying Awake at Night'; Roger Rothwell 'Another Prayer for Food'; Frederick Rackstraw (from John Marsh) 'Last Post'; Phillip Whitfield 'Day of Liberation, Bergen-Belsen, May 1945'; Robin Ivy 'Italy to Austria'; Victor West 'The Victors'; John Warry 'War Graves'; Edward Lowbury 'August 10th, 1945 – The Day After'; Norman Maxwell Dunn 'Let's Go Back'; F.A. Horn (from Mrs Irene Horn) 'Release Group Blues'; Ian Fletcher (from Lorraine Fletcher) 'Friends Gone'; Michael Armstrong 'The Meadow'.

Thanks are due to the following for kind permission to reproduce photographs:

Hulton-Deutsch Collection 23, 30; Robert Hunt Library 35, 67, 107, 115; Imperial War Museum 28, 38, 54, 57, 84, 88, 91, 103, 108, 111, 118, 136, 142; Peter Newark's Military Pictures 27; Novosti Information Agency 125; Popperfoto 17, 33, 75, 80, 131, 135; Topham Picture Library 60, 63, 99; United States Army photograph 76.